2003

How to Grow a Second Skin for Your Soul

For Those Who Feel

- *Hurt*
- *Judged*
- *Criticized*
- *Abandoned*
- *Invalidated*

When Someone Else

Acts Like a Jerk

by

Alisa S. Burgess, Ph.D.

THE OAKLEA PRESS

RICHMOND, VIRGINIA

FIRST EDITION
First Printing, August 2002

ISBN 1-892538-08-3

Front cover photograph of author by Scott Wall.

If your bookseller does not have this book in stock,
it can be ordered directly from the publisher.
More information can be found at the
Web site shown below,
or call our toll-free number.

The Oaklea Press
6912-B Three Chopt Road
Richmond, Virginia 23226

Voice: 1-800-295-4066
Facsimile: 1-804-281-5686
Email: Orders@OakleaPress.com

Web site: http://www.OakleaPress.com

DEDICATION

To Harold (Hal) Blajwas
You are the wind beneath my wings.

ACKNOWLEDGMENTS

My heartfelt appreciation extends to Hal Blajwas, my adored earth partner. Words cannot express the significant role you played in this process. Your love, support and patience enabled the vision for this book to become a reality. I am eternally grateful to you.

I wish to thank Stephen H. Martin, my extraordinary publisher and editor, whose shared vision enabled this book to become published. Thank you for your clairvoyant ability to see beyond the originally proposed title for this book and to value its content and message. And thank you for your superb editorial expertise. I feel extremely fortunate to have found just the right publisher and editor with whom to collaborate on this project.

I wish to thank Lewis Bostwick for his metaphysical teachings. I also wish to thank Diane Newman for her spiritual guidance throughout the years.

My sincere gratitude extends to Caroline Sikes for her technical assistance with reformatting this book on the computer and for altruistically offering one evening of her time to do so. My appreciation also extends to Paul Spiegel for his consultation on contracts and for his technical support.

I wish to thank Margret Robinson, Ph.D., my cherished friend and colleague. You are a true "yes" category person in my life. I also wish to thank Diane Zacher, Ph.D., Myrna Quan Holden, Ph.D., Annette Pont-Gwire, Ph.D., and Spencer Schein, Ph.D., who have been such wonderful colleagues and friends during the past fifteen years.

I wish to express my heartfelt appreciation to my revered

patients and students throughout the past fifteen years. I feel deeply privileged to have had the opportunity to share your journeys with you. You have in many ways, been my greatest teachers.

Finally, my heart extends to Lucille I. Burgess. I feel your love and enthusiasm from the heavens above.

CONTENTS

INTRODUCTION

This book was written for the openhearted and sensitive souls on this planet who are prone to losing their boundaries in relationships. Others may easily hurt you. And you may have difficulty expressing your true feelings and setting boundaries for yourself because you fear that others will react negatively towards you. You may fear, for instance, that if you speak your truth, others will become angry and abandon you, criticize, judge, invalidate or send you on a guilt trip.

You may find your "self" or soul imprisoned by dependency and the fear of others' negative reactions. If you are such a person, then *How to Grow a Second Skin for Your Soul* will emancipate your soul and guide you through the process of developing healthy boundaries and becoming solid within your "self."

"What if a man gain the whole world and lose his own soul?" asks one of the great spiritual masters. What is the price one pays for compromising his or her boundaries in order to maintain status quo? The price is immeasurable, for the loss of one's boundaries leads to the loss of one's self.

The inability to establish healthy boundaries leads to the common symptoms of depression, low self-esteem and discord in relationships. Unfortunately, a lack of healthy boundaries is a prevalent and detrimental ailment affecting millions of people's lives.

Without a solid core and the ability to set boundaries, one loses one's self, and will experience the anxiety of feeling "engulfed" or the depression of feeling "abandoned" in relationships. Moreover, without a "semi-permeable boundary" to filter out the negative energy while letting in the good, one loses one's centeredness, self-esteem and objectivity in relationships. You may then be susceptible to becoming regressed and reactive in your relationships with others.

The establishment of healthy boundaries is a quintessential element in developing a solid sense of self and in attaining the emotional and spiritual freedom that comes from being individuated. One is not born with healthy boundaries. One is not born with *any* boundaries, for that matter. On the path towards wholeness and ultimately enlightenment, one must journey through the gauntlet of life's experiences, where opportunities exist to develop both a protection from harmful energies and a filter for letting in positive energies. In the end, if one successfully builds a healthy, semi-permeable "bubble" which keeps out the bad and lets in the good, then, and only then, can one consistently open one's heart to all. For in this state of being, one is centered in one's core, and is impervious to "zings" and "blows" that would ordinarily throw someone off their center. One transcends unhealthy energy and stays in a space of peacefulness.

It is impossible to go directly from Point "A", which is the undifferentiated state of symbiosis at birth, to Point "E", which is to the solid, centered, individuated and open-hearted space of enlightenment. One must first travel sequentially through the building of a boundary, (Point "B"), the implementation of a filter (Point "C"), and the anchoring of one's core behind the now semi-permeable bubble (Point "D"). While some would argue that certain people such as Christ, Buddha, and some saints were born into this state of enlightenment without having gone through the steps in between, the vast majority of us humans must plod through life's

16

lessons and build the scaffolding and shields as we journey on the path towards enlightenment.

This book is your guide to do just that. Whether you are in the undifferentiated space of feeling like you have no boundaries or protection, whether you are jaded from pain and have built a fortress of protection to keep out the bad, or whether you have mastered the ability to open yourself to the good despite having endured deep pain, this book will guide you through the journey of establishing healthy boundaries and towards a state of peacefulness and sense of solidness in your core.

In this book, I propose a three-dimensional, conceptual approach to healing the past and moving you back into your body so that you can feel your emotions and use your feelings as your guide.

You will be guided in how to:

- Establish healthy boundaries where you feel protected in a transparent, semi-permeable "bubble-shield"
- Individuate and let go of energies that control or restrict one's spiritual freedom, making way for supportive and nurturing energies to enter your life
- Build a solid sense of self, enabling you to transcend negative emotions and overcome addictions
- Stay centered when triggers and assaults occur
- Transcend negativity and maintain a state of peacefulness within, and a state of acceptance towards others

As an evolutionary-oriented self-help book, *How to Grow a Second Skin for Your Soul* is also the first book to bridge psychological theory with metaphysical "tools" and concepts in order to guide you through the developmental process of individuation and towards the building of healthy boundaries. This book presents complicated psychological theories in the form of intuitive, metaphorical, fun and comprehensible language that it is intended to resonate with the experience and soul of the reader. Metaphysical concepts and visualization tools are incorporated throughout the book, giving you the means and guidelines for effectively handling negative encounters and triggers while maintaining your centeredness. Cases and examples are interspersed throughout the book illustrating common situations with which you, the reader, can readily identify.

How to Grow a Second Skin for Your Soul:

- Explains the origin of how one "loses one's self," and how one's defense mechanisms and addictions perpetuate the "disconnect" of the self
- Presents the process of healing and reconnection to one's self
- Introduces the concept of boundaries in relationship, the individuation process and "keeping out the bad," and the healing process of "letting in the good"
- Provides practical tools and strategies for dealing with negative people and interactions while staying centered
- Illustrates concepts and techniques for achieving flexible boundaries, healthy interactions and forgiveness in partnerships
- Presents metaphysical concepts and visualization tools for maintaining your center when triggers occur, for strengthening your core, for overcoming addictions, and for soothing your self
- Offers a series of practical exercises to assist you in staying solid within your self when invalidated by negative energy, to assist you in soothing your self, and to assist

you in becoming more familiar with your relationship
patterns and your core essence

In Part I, you will be guided through the individuation process
as you let go of energies that control or restrict your spiritual
freedom, making way for supportive and nurturing energies to enter
your life. In Part II, you will be guided in how to deal with harmful
as well as good energies as you are interacting with others in your
relationships and developing flexible boundaries. In Part III, you
will be introduced to a conceptual approach of visualizing energy,
which will then be used for learning tangible ways to maintain your
center and strengthen your core when triggers occur. Finally, in Part
IV, you will be guided in exercises to assist you in staying solid
within your self when you are invalidated by negative energies. In
addition, exercises are offered to assist you in becoming more
familiar with your relationship patterns, your desires and your core
essence.

In the end, you will be well on your way to safely loving all with
an open heart, as the Masters demonstrate. For you will have
healthy boundaries and clarity for truth, enabling you to transcend
harmful energies while having an open heart. For you will have
grown a "second skin for your soul." Enjoy the journey.

Part I
THE INDIVIDUATION PROCESS

Chapter 1
THE ORIGIN OF PAIN

You are about to embark on a wonderfully creative and visual journey that can transform your life. The journey into knowing your self well can pave the way for you to be able to successfully handle any outside trigger and thus, give you inner peace. All that is needed is your imagination, your presence and your heart. Let's start with the genesis of you.

Imagine in your mind's eye a representation of you as a gingerbread cookie cutout. Next, place a bubble "an arm's length" around the figure representing you. This bubble is your "space" or energy field.

"Your Bubble"

When you are born, all of your energy is flowing freely throughout your body and energy field. When you come out of the womb at birth, you are completely in "present time." You are not thinking about the past or future, but rather attending to the moment. When you are in present time and your energy is flowing freely throughout your body, you are feeling all of your emotions, and you are in "ease" with your self.

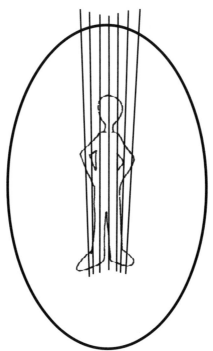

"Energy Flowing Freely Through Your Body"

Let us imagine that your brain and body is a perfect recording machine. Let us imagine that every experience you have ever lived through is recorded somewhere in your body.

Each experience has a memory and an emotion attached to it. If an experience occurs that is too painful or traumatic to feel at the time, the memory will be repressed into the unconscious, and you will disassociate or "leave your body" in order not to feel the pain.

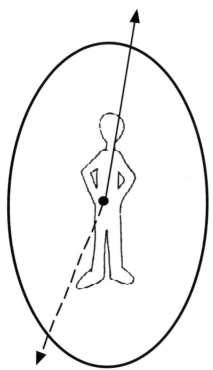

"Repression of a Memory and Leaving the Body"

After a while, you will enter back into your body and run your energy throughout your body, *except* for the space in your body where the painful experience was recorded. That space becomes like a frozen piece of energy in your body. Then another painful experience occurs. For instance, suppose a parent divorced and left the family. If the experience was too painful for your little child body to experience, you will again repress the memory into your unconscious, and you will leave your body so as not to feel the pain. When you again re-enter your body, you will run energy throughout your body *except* for the places where the painful experiences were recorded.

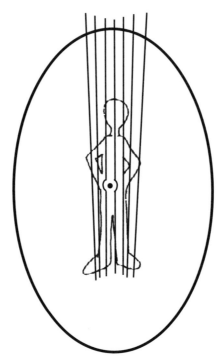

"Energy Flowing Freely Through Your Body, Except Where a Frozen, Repressed Memory Resides"

Over time, you may have many frozen pain pockets in your energy field. You may have so many, in fact, that you begin to live most of the time disassociated from your body and from your pain. In other words, you begin to live "out of your body" most of the time. This state makes you feel like you are in a constant fog, and you will have difficulty concentrating because you are not present and in your body. This state is depression.

The frozen pockets of experience can harbor other feeling states as well. For instance, if some experiences cause extreme anxiety (e.g. a death of a parent), and the anxiety was too painful to experience, the person will disassociate from the pain and from the body, and will repress the memory into the unconscious in order to avoid feeling the anxiety.

Chapter 2
ADDICTIONS AND DEFENSE MECHANISMS

In order to say "out of the body" so as not to feel the pain, the person will develop addictions and/or defense mechanisms. Addictions can be "wonderful" anesthesia keeping one from feeling her/his feelings.

People use many forms of substances such as alcohol, food, nicotine, cocaine, marijuana, prescription pain medications and heroin to deaden the pain. They can use various behavior patterns such as bingeing and purging, shopping, gambling, using the computer, overworking, and "co-dependency," such as focusing on others, in order not to feel one's own pain. Any behavior or use of substance that is used to take one away from experiencing one's feelings or from being present in the body is harmful to the person, in that these behaviors perpetuate a disassociative state, which keeps them disconnected from their feelings and from their souls. One therefore becomes out of affinity with his/her self.

The "Understanding Mode"

Besides addictive behaviors, people can also use defense mechanisms to keep them "out of the body" so as not to feel the pain. A particularly common defense mechanism I witness in my practice is that of being "too understanding." I call this the "understanding mode."

People often make excuses for others' ill-intentioned or reprehensible behavior at the expense of feeling their own hurt or anger. They defend themselves, and respond to my prodding to examine their true feelings towards the offender by saying that they are being "forgiving," and/or brought up to be religious/spiritual. They override their hurt or angry feelings and believe they are the healthier and more spiritual for it. Yet if they are denying their pain, then they are in a "pseudo-enlightened" space, because their "understanding mode" is serving as a defense mechanism keeping them from feeling their own pain towards the situation.

Co-Dependency

Co-dependency is another common behavioral defense mechanism. If one focuses on healing the other person's problems instead of focusing upon one's own problems, if one focuses upon changing the other person instead of changing themselves, or if one focuses upon protecting the other person (e.g. colluding with an alcoholic spouse's destructive habit by making excuses to the spouse's boss about the alcohol-related absences), then the behavior can detract from the frustrating or painful feelings that are residing within him or her self. She/he may believe and feel that she/he is being altruistic and helpful by focusing upon another. Yet again, if the behavior takes one away from his/her own pain, then it is a defense mechanism.

I encounter a lot of resistance in my practice to people not wanting to "let go" of control. They resist allowing the person they are trying to "help" to live their own life, learn their own lessons and hit their own "rock bottom." The first point I make is that it is not their job to play "God" and attempt to steer another person's course. I point out that if they interfere with another person's Life Path lessons, then they could be incurring negative karma by attempting to control a situation and thereby, attempting to play God.

It is entirely possible to be loving and supportive from afar without interfering and meddling with another person's Life Path. If a person is not a dependent adult or severely intellectually challenged, then it is desirable to refrain from rescuing or "saving" a person from falling or from feeling their own pain. As every parent knows, it can be excruciating to watch your toddler physically fall down on her knees and bottom while learning to walk. Yet if you interfere and prevent her from falling, she will never learn to walk on her own. You can be there for emotional support and soothing when your babies cry during the trial and error. And the same principle holds for others in your life. You can support your friends and family from afar without interfering with their Path and from the experiences they need to feel.

The second point I explore is the person's fear of the consequences that will ensue if they do not "help" by controlling the situation. This exploration brings the person into many of the feelings they are defending against. These feelings are usually the energy that is controlling them and keeping them from being spiritually free. They feel that if they do not help or control the other person's situation, then they will feel extremely guilty, and/or feel that they are "abandoning" the person. Or they may feel that they would anger the other person, or be abandoned, punished, criticized, ostracized, judged, or any number of other reactions if they do not comply and "help." They are essentially prisoners, controlled by their own fear of the consequences if they rescind their "helpfulness."

They are not spiritually free or individuated. They will stuff their feelings, often unbeknownst to themselves, using addictions such as food, pills, drugs, shopping, starving, gambling etc. to keep them from feeling their own pain. If they *were* to feel their pain, they would then have to do something about speaking up for themselves, and they would have to endure the energy that may well be hurled at them for not continuing to "help" the other person.

Other Defense Mechanisms

There are several other defense mechanisms that people often use to keep themselves "out of their bodies" and away from feeling their own pain. Some examples of other commonly used defense mechanisms are denial, rationalization (making a "silk purse" out of a "sow's ear"), rumination (worrying), intellectualization, obsessive-compulsiveness, passive-aggressiveness (withholding from someone in order to aggravate or punish), reaction-formation (acting the opposite of how one feels in order to be liked or to be socially acceptable), splitting (seeing someone as all good or all bad because it is too painful to tolerate both emotions simultaneously towards one person), somatization (manifesting bodily symptoms as a result of emotional pain), and displacement (directing emotions towards less threatening persons/objects).

Chapter 3
THE HEALING PROCESS

The healing process begins when one removes their addictions and defense mechanisms. By doing so, one begins to enter their body and one begins to run their energy through the frozen pockets of pain.

When you begin to run your energy through a particular pocket of pain, several things start to happen. You will begin to feel the original emotion and release some of the charge it has. If you stay with the emotion long enough, the memory associated with the pain will begin to surface out of the unconscious.

The memory will be in the form of a "picture" or series of pictures. Over time, if you allow yourself to feel, then all the memories that were repressed begin to come into your consciousness where they can be felt, released, and integrated into your being. You then will be bringing the frozen, past-time energy into present time, and you will no longer experience big gaps in your life memories. Your energy will be flowing freely through every space in your body, and you will be in affinity with your self.

Wells of Pain

Imagine each frozen picture as a well of pain. Each well may have one to several defense mechanisms or addictions "protecting" you from feeling the pain. Once the defense mechanism or addiction is removed, you will descend into the well and feel the pain deeply for a long period of time. Eventually, say a day or two and sometimes longer, you will surface out of the well and out of the regressed-feeling state.

The next time you either chose to enter into the pain, or the pain is triggered by a present-time event, you will again descend into the well of pain. This time, however, you will not go down as far nor will you stay down as long as you did the first time. The third time, you will not descend quite as far as you did the second time down, and your stay in the well will be shorter still.

With each descent, you progressively go in and out of the well of pain in shorter and shallower intervals. Ultimately, the well becomes a scar with little pain left to discharge. The scar will always be there, perhaps, but it will not cause the pain that it once did when it was an open wound, and you will not have to defend against the pain.

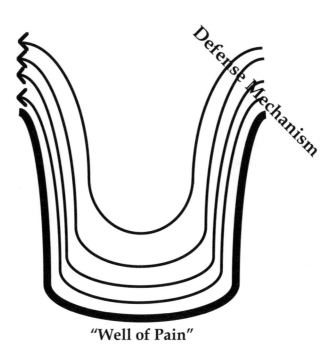

"Well of Pain"

Some new patients reported that they have "felt their pain all of their lives," and that the pain never seems to go away. Upon close analysis, however, I inevitably discover that they have certain defense mechanisms that keep their pain "just enough at bay" so that they never consciously allow themselves to feel the heart of the emotion. Thus the pain is never released. Their defense mechanisms keep the pain at a sub-level so that it is enough to feel, but not enough to be released.

The journey into the wells of pain can take place through several pathways. One is through the conscious choice of feeling the pain. You can arrive at a well through meditation and staying with the feelings to evoke the memories. Secondly, you can remove the defense mechanisms or addictions and feel what surfaces over time during withdrawal. A third way to access a well of pain is through watching a movie that resonates with your pain, thereby triggering emotions and memories within your self. Yet the most common way to step into the well of pain is by interacting with people, which can result in triggering your pictures. The following will explain.

Pictures and Transferences

Imagine again the gingerbread man representation of you. Next, imagine all of the pictures from your past with frozen pieces of emotion attached to them. Visualize these pictures residing within your body. If someone or something in present time reminds you consciously or unconsciously of a frozen picture/event in your space, that picture will reverberate, and you will feel the original emotion that was attached to the picture.

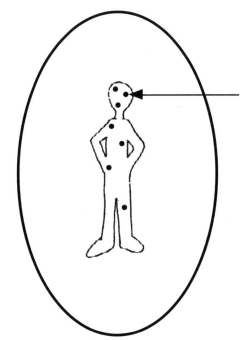

**"Outside Energy Triggering a Picture
in Your Space"**

It is called a "transference" when you actually transfer your frozen, past-time feelings onto the present-time event. The goal is to be able to separate the feelings that are coming from the past from the feelings that are coming from the present. Usually, the majority of the charge from the emotion is coming from the past, and only a small percentage of the emotional charge can be attributed to the present.

Pictures are triggered every day by interactions with our environment. Since each of us is made up from our own unique experiences, our lenses of the world are unique to us. Some of us will have pictures triggered by an event or person while that same event or person has no triggering effect upon our neighbor. This is due to the fact that our neighbor does not have a similar experience or picture that is charged in his energy field.

There should be no negative judgment of yourself because your emotions are triggered by someone or something when those of others are not. Your pictures are unique to you. They make you who you are.

When you are triggered, however, you do not want to act out the emotion that is attached to the picture. The goal instead, is to be aware of your picture and the emotion attached to it, feel the emotion internally, thereby releasing some of the charge, and then return to present time by separating out the transference. You may then decide whether you want to share what it is you are feeling and where the feeling is coming from. It is best to share these feelings from a neutral and centered space, rather than from a reactive space. An example of coming from a neutral, centered space would be, "The hurt that I am feeling as a result of the comment you just made triggered the same feeling I had as a child when my father criticized me." An example of coming from a reactive space would be, "You are such a jerk" or "You are just like my father."

Our pain pictures are like magnets that attract just the right type of person or situation to trigger the pain. Our pain will be triggered again and again *until we learn to become neutral to the trigger* and heal and release the original pain. We become neutral to the trigger by allowing ourselves to feel the pain from the past that is triggered by the present, and to remember and reexperience the original feeling state and memory. You can heal the pain by embracing the pain and releasing the energy over time. You will then be able to separate the present trigger from the past memory, you will be able to see the present trigger clearly and accurately without the past emotion tainting the situation, and you will be able to observe yourself feeling the emotions without plummeting into the emotions.

Emotion as "Energy in Motion"

People are commonly afraid to experience their feelings. While the healing process sounds good in theory, people tend to resist feeling negative affect. When I explore my patients' reasoning for wanting to resist the descent into the "wells of pain," I have heard some say it would feel like "death," or they would fear going "crazy." I reply to their responses with the following metaphor.

Emotion is merely "energies in motion," (Bradshaw, 1996). "E – motion," (Bradshaw, 1996). Everything in the universe is energy. You are energy. Every cell in your body is energy moving in wave patterns. Everything is energy moving in wave patterns.

Why are you afraid of a little energy moving through your body? Take for instance the color red. Red is a slow wave on the color spectrum. You may have heard of the expression, "feeling red with anger." Imagine the slow wave energy pattern of the red vibration running through your body when you are feeling anger. Anger is just a vibration, and it will dissipate if you allow the energy to flow through you. If you resist the energy, however it will be stored, and it will accumulate force that must be dealt with at a later time. (The topic of anger is discussed in Chapter Four).

Likewise, you may have heard of the expression, "feeling 'yellow with fear'." Fear could then be seen as merely a yellow color vibration that has a slightly faster wavelength than red. In feeling "green with envy," green is a slightly faster wavelength than yellow. In feeling "blue" with sadness, blue is a faster wavelength than green. Why are we afraid to feel a little energy flowing through our bodies? All emotion is "energy in motion." You need to feel in order to heal.

Chapter 4
BOUNDARIES

Your Bubble

Imagine that you have a transparent and semi-permeable bubble around you. This bubble is the outer layer of your energy field. It completely surrounds you. It is above you, beside you, in front of you, behind you, and beneath your feet. It allows you to observe the world from behind its transparent shield.

Your bubble is like a semi-permeable membrane, in that it shields you from unwanted, negative energy while letting in good energy. The key is in recognizing which energies are harmful to your energy field and which energies are loving and good.

Health

Basically, two types of energy exist in the universe: Yours, and everyone else's. Only your energy should be inside your bubble. Everyone else's energy should be outside of your bubble. You are healthy and "in ease" with your body when you are running only your own energy in your space. You are in "dis-ease" with your body when others' energy in your bubble blocks the ease and flow of your own energy in your space.

Disease (dis-ease) occurs when either "frozen" energy or "foreign" energy is in your space. Frozen energy is energy that results from stagnant memories from your past that have not been consciously addressed or felt. Foreign energy is energy that is put into your space by either a person's ill-meaning intention, such as abuse, or by a person's well-meaning intention, such as engulfing you or smothering you with their love.

Foreign energy can also accumulate in your space when you are healing others' pain by bringing it into your space to heal. There is another healthier, and less co-dependent way to heal others' pain rather than by taking their pain into your space to heal. It has to do with *sympathizing*, or having compassion for the other person's pain, rather than *empathizing*, or feeling their pain as if it were your own. Remember the previous discussion on co-dependency, and allow people to have their own pain and their own life path lessons. You will be happier and healthier if you focus only on your own energy.

No, Maybe, and Yes Category People

There are three categories of people on this planet: The "No's", the "Maybe's", and the "Yes's." The "no" category people are people who are harmful to your energy field because they cause you pain. They are the people who are entrenched in their dysfunction, and who are not willing to grow on an emotional and spiritual level. They are the people who get defensive, and who blame you and project their negative feelings onto you when you express your feelings in a neutral and sharing fashion. If you feel invalidated, judged, criticized, punished, guilt-tripped, silenced, cut-off or abandoned when you are attempting to share your truth from a centered space, it is a good indication that you are interacting with a "no" category person.

The "maybe" category person is someone who vacillates between being receptive to your feelings on some occasions, and being defensive and reactive to your feelings on other occasions. These people have at least some awareness of their volatile behavior and reactions, and they are usually participating in some type of therapy, spiritual or recovery program, or self-help path. These people can behave like a "no" category person, in that they can get defensive and throw negative energy at you when you share your feelings from a centered and non-attacking space, but they can then come around to a centered and receptive space within a short to medium time frame (i.e. hours to a day or two). They are probably the most difficult category to deal with because you like these people, but they can cause you pain.

The key to dealing with the "maybe" category people is in learning to close your heart down a bit when they are in an attacking and defensive mode, and opening your heart when they are back on their center. It can be challenging to master the malleability of one's heart, because love can be "blind", and one tends to feel guilty if she/he temporarily shuts down the heart center in order to see the situation clearly. Initially, the goal is to be able to stay in the center of your head, where you can see the situation clearly (6th chakra) while opening or closing down the heart (4th chakra) according to the energies being directed at you. Eventually however, you will be able to keep your heart open all the time, and let your bubble protect and shield you from their energy. In the end, you must stay centered and aware at all times when dealing with a "maybe" category person.

The "yes" category people are those who are effortless to be around. They neither drain your energy nor make you feel off-centered. These people are on their spiritual path. They do not judge you or withdraw their love from you. They allow you to have your feelings and to express yourself because they are interested in your feelings and want to understand you. They can agree to disagree with you without making you feel invalidated, criticized or judged. When they offer constructive feedback, it is with a loving and non-judgmental energy. You feel receptive and trusting of them because they do not want to control you or make you lose your self. You can have your heart open around these people because they do not throw "daggers" into your heart. These are the type of people you want in your life. And this is the type of person you want to become 100% of the time.

Your Personal Space

Imagine once again that you are in the center of your bubble. Your personal space is all the space inside your bubble. The outer membrane of your bubble demarcates your personal space and becomes your boundary. The radius from your center to the outer edge is usually about three feet, so that three feet of space completely surrounds you -- above you, beside you, in front of you, behind you, and beneath you.

It is your birthright to have your bubble around you with a comfortable amount of space for yourself in your bubble. In a perfect world, your bubble is respected, and no one caves it in with his/her energy. Likewise, you are not caving in others' bubbles. When everyone has healthy boundaries and no one is caving in others' bubbles, it feels like heaven. When someone pierces your bubble by invalidating, judging, criticizing or insulting you in some way and you are unable to become "senior" to the energy, you "lose your space." Likewise, your bubble caves in and you lose your space if someone engulfs, abuses, controls, manipulates or forces you to compromise yourself to become a doormat.

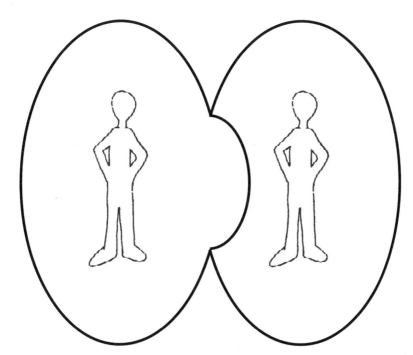

"A Boundary Being Caved In"

If your space has been caved in, it is your birthright to reset your boundary membrane to its original scrimmage line in order to have your personal space around you. Resetting a boundary involves speaking up for yourself and calling the offender on the energy that she/he attempted to control you with.

For many, it is often difficult to know when their bubble has been caved in because they are so used to being the doormat. How then does one break the cycle of the "doormat syndrome?" What is the energy you need to feel in order recognize that your boundary has been violated? The energy you need to feel is probably the most controversial energy of all. It is that of anger.

Anger: The Dignity Emotion

Anger is the "dignity emotion." At first glance, this statement appears to be an oxymoron because many of our religious and social upbringings label anger as "undignified." However, anger is the indicative feeling that is evoked when your bubble has been violated.

In his beautifully written and elucidating book, *Bradshaw On: The Family - A New Way of Creating Solid Self-Esteem,* John Bradshaw states, "Anger is essential as the core energy of our strength" (1996). He says, "Without my energy (called anger), I am powerless to uphold my dignity and self-worth," (Bradshaw, 1996). The following scenario is meant to cast the emotion of anger in a different and favorable light.

When we are born, we have all of the emotions in our repertoire to feel as humans. As babies, we feel happiness when we are given loving attention, we feel content when we are fed, we cry when we are wet, we laugh when we are amused and we get angry when our toys are taken away from us.

Imagine that you are three and a half years old and you are playing with your teddy bear. Then your younger brother, sister or playmate comes along and swipes your beloved companion away from you. You cry, "Give me back my teddy bear!" You feel angered by the fact that your property has been taken away from you, and you fight for your dignity by speaking up about it. You defend your boundary and maintain your dignity.

How then does one lose her/his ability to defend her/his boundary throughout the years? What can possibly happen to de-program anger out of one's emotional repertoire?

In the above scenario, imagine that your mother, father, or schoolteacher (who is quite intimidating as an authority figure) comes onto the scene and scolds you, saying, "Wipe that anger off your face! Never get angry at your brother/sister/playmate again!"

So the next time you are playing with your teddy bear and your sibling/playmate takes your bear away and caves your boundary in, you acquiesce and implode because your anger has been squelched. You no longer have the energy of the dignity emotion to defend your turf, and you become a doormat for others to step on.

Later on, each time someone caves your boundary in, you stuff the anger, and perhaps drink, eat, smoke, shop, or turn the anger inwards to become depressed. (The psychodynamic definition for depression is "anger turned inward"). Or you may use defense mechanisms such as denial, reaction formation (i.e. acting the opposite of how you really feel) or being overly understanding. Your personal space is violated, and you become so used to it that you don't even notice it after a while. You accept that this is how you are supposed to feel, yet you do not know why you have low self-esteem and depression.

Reawakening the Dignity Emotion

The dignity emotion can be re-awakened however, when the energy that caves in your boundary becomes so painful that you finally reach your point of intolerance. For some, it means being abused so badly that the predicament becomes a life or death situation, and one's life force wins, mobilizing the forces within to escape. For others, it may be the one last straw that "broke the camel's back." And for others, it may be the self-actualized realization that the way they are behaving is not working for them anymore. When the membrane of your bubble is caved in so close to you that it finally gets pushed to the brink, you will find your anger.

Visualize the following analogy. Your bubble is your spaceship that you drive through life. Hopefully, you are in the driver's seat of your spaceship. If you are in the passenger seat or back seat, others are enabled to climb into your ship and drive it for you. The gasoline that fuels the spaceship and mobilizes your forces in many cases is anger.

Picture the anger as red in color. In a perfect world, you will access your anger and *feel* the red energy, but will modulate the unbridled force of the anger by "running" a cooler, blue energy. This cooler and channeled shade of energy, which is fueled by the force of the anger, enables you to speak up for yourself and reset your boundary in a neutral and dignified manner. In other words, it is *not* desirable to explode or express rage towards someone. However, modulating anger is next to impossible to do at first because your anger has been locked up for years.

Taking the Lid Off the Pressure Cooker

Imagine your anger has been stored in a pressure cooker since the time when your parents, teachers and others squelched this energy. Over the years, it has accumulated energy, and over the years, the acquired defense mechanisms have kept the lid on the anger.

Then one day you remove the lid, or the lid cracks, and out leaps the unbridled genie in the bottle. Like a pendulum that swings from one extreme to the other, the anger will swing to the opposite, reactive position before settling into the middle, gray region. To quote Sir Isaac Newton's third law of motion, "Every action has an equal and opposite reaction." So is it true for the emancipation of your anger.

You cannot expect yourself to be able to speak up for yourself in a perfectly neutral and dignified manner the first time you access your anger because it has been stored up for so long where it has been accumulating energy. When you first start getting in touch with your anger, you may *feel* like a raged "Medusa" as the anger swings to the far end of the pendulum. You may actually step on some toes by snapping or being reactive. Eventually however, you will become comfortable enough with the energy to modulate the anger and bridle it with reason, moving the anger and pendulum towards the center, gray region.

The Medusa Phase

Many people strongly resist the inevitable "Medusa" phase, which coincides with familiarizing themselves with their anger. The resistance is particularly strong in persons coming from alcoholic and dysfunctional families and in persons coming from religions that believe anger is a sin. These people may erroneously believe that anger is destructive and equated with rage. However, when one grasps the concept that without anger, one has no boundaries, and when one realizes that anger is the dignity emotion, which is different than rage, then the process of awakening the anger becomes less threatening to them. One has to feel the power and force of this emotion and become familiar with its' (often unbridled) energy before gaining mastery over it. If one uses his/her rigid and punitive inner voice of the super-ego to clamp down one's anger, then it will not be possible to embrace and employ this constructive and healthy dignity energy.

In the beginning phase of accessing your anger, you may feel like you are a monster. The energy you are putting out is not, however, nearly as intense as it feels from your perspective inside your space.

This notion is consistently reconfirmed in groups I lead, where one feels out of control, yet the other group members' feedback is that they did not feel the person's anger was excessive. Rather, they felt that the energy was merely different for that person because it was out of character for the person to be angry.

There is a lot of energy at work, however, that would prevent one from activating one's self to re-set his/her birthright boundary. This energy is "control" energy, and it may have power over you. The process of individuating is the process of freeing yourself from the fear of the energy that has control over you.

Chapter 5

INDIVIDUATION: BECOMING FREE
OF THE ENERGY THAT CONTROLS YOU

The energy that controls you may come in a variety of forms. Imagine that you are in the center of your bubble and someone caves in your bubble. If you are unable to speak up for yourself and activate a boundary, then there is "control" energy operating to squelch your anger and your ability to speak up for yourself. If this energy comes from your past experiences, you would regress into the space where the energy was frozen and introject the control energy into your psyche as if the incident were real in present time. An example would be a parent punishing you in the past for getting angry. You feel paralyzed in present time because you introject the past parental punishment, and you feel as if the punishment is going to happen to you in the present. Or, the control energy may indeed be real in present time. In which case, for example, you might experience a negative reaction from another, such as being abandoned, if you speak up for yourself.

You keep quiet because this control energy puts "fear" in your space. You may fear, and rightly so, that if you reset your boundary, the person may react by judging you, criticizing you, abandoning you, turning others against you, punishing you, cutting you off financially or otherwise, intimidating you, making you feel guilty, getting angry towards you, or physically hurting you. The key is to say your truth, protect yourself emotionally and physically with your bubble, and if necessary, seek support and protection from others (e.g. the police), and be able to tolerate the disconnect in order to free yourself from their chains of control.

You are "spiritually free" when you no longer fear the reactions of people when you activate your self. In this space of individuation and spiritual freedom, people no longer have authority over you. You feel equal to anyone and everyone as a citizen of this planet.

In addition, you are spiritually free when people no longer have the ability to threaten your sense of self and self-esteem because you are solid and can find validation within yourself. And you claim your birthright of entitlement to own your own perspective and truth.

Emptying the Cup:
Ridding Yourself of the "No" Category People

The process of individuating and becoming spiritually free is perhaps the most difficult process with which we as human beings can be faced. Without a doubt, it is the single most common issue people bring with them into my practice. The issue may initially be disguised as an addiction, depression, a dysfunctional relationship, or any other outwardly visible complaint, but the underlying core issue invariably turns out to be that of "individuation."

To begin to speak up for yourself to those who have had authority and control over you is easier said than done. It is equally as difficult to cut the cords from people who drain your energy field due to their dysfunction, addiction, or manipulation and guilt. If people want to have power and control over you, or if they drain you and manipulate you so they won't have to take responsibility for themselves, then they are in the "no" category, and it would be in your best interest to reestablish the boundaries with these people on your own terms. If they throw negative energy at you because you are reestablishing the boundaries by speaking up for yourself, (e.g. they punish, judge or abandon you), then you may need to "empty your cup" of these people and let go of the unhealthy relationship.

As you let go of "no" category individuals, you are emptying your cup of dysfunctional people and making room for the "yes" category people to enter your life. The "yes" category people will generally *not* be attracted to you when your cup is filled with "no" category people because the "no" category energy of others surrounds you and oppresses you, making you invisible to their "yes" category higher vibration energy. If you are depressed or have chaos around you, it can *repel* higher vibration from you.

As you begin to shift your energy field and activate your boundaries, thereby creating a healthy bubble around you, the "no" category people will likely begin to hurl even *stronger* negative energy at you. It is their conscious or unconscious attempt to cave your bubble in and make you acquiesce so that they keep you under their thumb or for themselves. Like a crab trying to escape from a pot with other crabs in it, as the crab crawls up towards the top of the pot, the other crabs try to pull the crab back down.

Here is a similar analogy. Imagine that you are in a rocket ship that is taking off from earth. As the rocket ship exits the earth's gravitational field, the ship shakes ferociously. If you can endure the shaking despite the discomfort, the ship will eventually exit the pull of the earth's gravitational field and float smoothly and freely into space.

Your spiritual fortitude will be tested during the ferocious shaking of your spaceship, when your "no" category relationship is hurling negative energy in full force in attempt to hold you back.

While the reactions of "no" people to your new boundaries may be harsh, you must tolerate their negative energy and the aloneness that may ensue in order to escape their control.

Enduring the Aloneness:
The Existential Crisis

Severing a relationship can be excruciatingly painful and the aloneness may be almost unbearable. I liken this feeling of aloneness to that of "floating out in the universe without an umbilical cord tethering you back to 'Mother Earth'." We are forced to enter our own "existential crisis" and feel the terror and pain of our separateness. As existentialist philosophers have ruminated upon, we must all face the feeling that we come into the world alone and that ultimately we die alone.

This condition is universal. All humans must ultimately come to terms with their existential aloneness as a prerequisite to feeling whole within themselves and then one with all. If a person does not come to terms with his/her existential aloneness, that person will need to defend against this feeling throughout life, without reaching a place where they feel whole and spiritually free.

Let us suppose the relationship that you need to sever is a long-term marriage. Suppose that the marriage is dysfunctional, in that you are not spiritually free, but instead are either being abused, manipulated, controlled, or oppressed. Nevertheless, you are used to the relationship and you have grown dependent upon the connection, believing that the dysfunctional connection is better than no connection. Next, suppose that life takes its natural course and you become increasingly unhappy. You defend against the unhappiness about your inability to activate your boundaries. You do this by either eating, shopping, or becoming addicted to something. Next, suppose that your addiction prompted you to seek therapy, and through guidance, you get in touch with the feelings that you had pushed aside due to your fear of the oppressor.

After removing the defense mechanisms and experiencing your feelings, you realize that you can no longer squelch your feelings, and must activate your boundaries with your spouse. When you initially activate yourself and speak up when criticized or abused, your spouse reacts with anger. Although you are fearful, you endure and continue to set your boundaries. If he/she is not willing to grow and allow you your freedom, he/she will use even more negative energy to keep you in the familiar backed-down position.

You will now have reached a crossroad. You may be financially dependent or emotionally dependent upon your spouse, and the thought of leaving may be extremely frightening. Yet the thought of staying may be increasingly constricting and deadening. The Universe, or Providence, as it is sometimes called, usually intervenes to cause what needs to happen to actually occur so that your course can be corrected. Either the oppression and abuse becomes so dangerous or unbearable that you have no choice but to leave, or your addiction becomes so severe that you have to activate yourself.

You now find yourself clinging to the relationship as a final defense against feeling the abandonment depression and feeling of aloneness. From where do these feelings originate? And why do so many of us feel like infants that are helpless to leave situations that are so harmful to us?

Early Developmental Phases

These feelings stem from developmental arrests that occur very early in our development. The feelings of intolerable anxiety and depression that ensue when a connection is severed stem from the stages in our infancy when we grow and separate from our primary caretaker, our mother or her surrogate. The following discussion is based upon the work of Margaret Mahler (1972), an object relations theorist, whose work involved the developmental stages of infancy and early childhood.

The initial phase of infancy development is "symbiosis," where we are "one with mother." When we come out of the womb, we are a bundle of unconscious energy still connected to the womb that housed us for so long. As we rest upon mother's chest, we feel a oneness with her and with her heartbeat. It is an "oceanic" feeling of bliss, and this oceanic bliss is often associated with the initial "honeymoon" phase during the beginning of a relationship.

The next phase is "differentiation" where we begin to differentiate between "me" and "not me." You are carried around by mother and need her for survival, yet you feel separate from her as well. You play with her necklace and look into her face, knowing it is separate from you and your body. Yet you are riding on her grounding cord and dependent upon her.

Often times in adult relationships, we relinquish our own grounding cord and become dependent on the other. It feels nice to trust and lean on, as it taps into the "healthy dependency" phase of our infancy where we are helpless, and need our mother's grounding to take care of us. Yet giving up our grounding cord in adult relationships may put us in a precarious position in the future of that relationship, as you shall see.

Next comes the "practicing" phase and the "rapprochement"

phase of crawling and toddling, where you are safe in mother's maternal orbit of energy, yet you are also discovering the world. According to James Masterson (1975), another leading forerunner in the field of object relations theory, the interaction between mother and child is so important during these phases in relationship to individuation issues. Mother must be there emotionally and physically for a child to feel secure, yet mother must not be too engulfing or the child will seek to distance him or herself, fear the connection and the losing of one's self.

Let's say you are fourteen months old and mama is in sight. You go off and explore somewhere and feel a sense of wonderment with the world and a wonderful sense of freedom. Then you start to become a little frightened at the thought of being all alone, as the metaphorical umbilical cord stretches too far and becomes severed. So you check back over your shoulder and turn around and see mama in the distance. You immediately feel relieved and run back to mama.

She hugs you and you feel safe, but after a while you start to feel suffocated. You fidget and fuss your way out of her arms and toddle off again. You feel a wonderful sense of freedom again. But then you start to get scared and check back, see mama in the distance, feel relieved and run back to her. This interplay between individuation/freedom and safety/security serves to shape our personalities and our relationships with others. Mama's ability to tolerate baby's separation from her as well as her ability to soothe, comfort and be there for baby is critical to the development of a healthy individuation process. Her soothing also allows you to eventually anchor yourself with your own grounding cord, as you internalize her soothing to soothe yourself when you are alone.

Let's take a look at another situation where you are around

mother and wander off to explore your environment. Initially, it feels wonderful as you are wandering out "into space" with your "umbilical cord" tethering you to mama. You then start to feel scared because of too much separation, and you check back to see where she is. To your alarm and utter panic, she is not there. She may have wondered off into another part of the house to talk on the phone. Or, in extreme circumstances, she may have actually abandoned you, severing the cord that grounded you into her grounding. This feeling may have been too anxiety-provoking for your little body to handle and feel, so you may have repressed the memory into the unconscious and left your body so as not to feel the abandonment. A single traumatic abandonment episode may be severe enough to cause a profound effect (e.g. a sudden death of a parent). More frequently, the fear is patterned by a series of physical and emotional abandonment episodes, such as a parent's chronic lateness in picking you up from day care, or a mother's ambivalence and periodic emotional withdrawal. Then you become insecure, clingy, or distrusting of someone being there for you. When these feelings get retriggered by a present-time relationship ending, the sheer panic of being alone, and the feeling as if you are "floating out in the universe without an umbilical cord" comes flooding in. You then feel the intensity of the emotion that you were unable to feel when you had a baby body, and it was too much for you to tolerate. Your grounding cord was not anchored into the earth to give you your own sense of security and soothing, and when you are severed from mama, it evokes panic.

Likewise, let's say mama was overprotective and would not let you explore your "universe" or go too far away from her. You end up feeling suffocated, terrified of losing your sense of self and being "merged" with her. To defend against the terror of losing your self and being engulfed, you distance yourself and become aloof. In present time, you may fear intimacy because it triggers the primitive fear of becoming engulfed by a larger force. Either you may become so aloof that you keep everyone at arm's length, or the opposite may occur. You may have difficulty setting limits for yourself in present time so that you actually do feel engulfed, which recreates the original engulfed state. You may feel that if you do set limits to create space for yourself, your partner will become so hurt or angry that he/she will leave, or your boss will fire you, etc.

How then, does one overcome the sheer terror of having no grounding cord? How does one overcome the notion that it is better to be oppressed and abused by a "no" category partner (or anyone else for that matter), who offers a false sense of grounding, than to feel their own emptiness and terror as a prerequisite to finding and owning their own grounding cord?

The answer comes from allowing yourself to *feel* the terror because most, if not all of it is coming from the past, when you really were too young to take care of yourself. The feelings come from a preverbal period of time when you were between birth and two years old, before you had a language to describe how you were feeling. That is why it is so difficult to put words to how you are feeling. It is also why the feelings are so overwhelming, because indeed they were overwhelming when you were an infant and were utterly helpless and dependent and in need of others to soothe you.

In present time, however, you are perfectly okay. You are fully able to take care of yourself. Only fear (and therefore excuses) gets in your way of taking care of yourself. You must access the nurturing parent part of yourself and soothe the frightened infant part of yourself. And the adult "you" must anchor your own grounding cord into your "real," eternal mother, who is Mother

Earth, for she will always be there under your feet to offer grounding to you.

It is during this time in the transformational process when many of my patients wish for a pill or medication to take the pain away. While I give people the option to take medication, I strongly encourage them to stay with the emotion so that they can access the frozen energy they have locked up for years, and so they can retrieve and reclaim the split off parts of their souls. Medication may dampen the pain, but it may also actually curtail the process of feeling these early emotional states. It may be better to give yourself permission to feel during this period. If you allow yourself to be okay with feeling a bit out of sorts and not perfectly "on top of your game" as you go through this process, the rewards on the other side can be priceless, for you will reclaim your soul and your spiritual freedom in the end. (Note: As always, please consult with your doctor or mental health care professional regarding medication, as circumstances differ from person to person, and you may indeed, be a candidate for medication.)

Keeping Out the "Bad":
The Incubation Period and Getting to Know Your Self

During the process of individuating from a "no" category person (e.g. a partner, parent or boss), you will be shifting your boundaries. Your bubble will be strengthening as you are learning to "keep out the bad," and you will be activating your self by setting limits, speaking your truth and saying "no." You will also be feeling the intense pain from the early years as you feel the aloneness and anchor your self into the earth with your own grounding cord.

I call this phase the "incubation" period, and liken it to an embryo whose shell is gelling but not quite hardened. This is a period to turn inward and to really get to know your self. As long as you are alone, you may as well enjoy yourself, and enjoy getting to know your own likes and dislikes. This is an ideal time to practice meditation and to consciously direct your focus towards the frozen pain pockets of your past in order to feel and heal. Others find their own meditative space through activities such as long-distance running or throwing pots in a ceramic studio. As long as you are creating a space to be alone with your thoughts and feelings, then you are anchoring your self to your soul.

Resist the urge to jump back into another relationship right away. Also resist the urge to defend against the pain by using any one of your defense mechanisms or addictions. To do so will be to curtail the transformational process, and you will be attracting the same dysfunctional energy into your life that you had before.

This is also a good time to buy three journals. One journal will be used for continuing to process your feelings and to interpret your night dreams. The second journal will be used for visualizing and creating your "ideal life" and all the things you want to have in it. You can also use this journal for writing an ongoing "gratitude list" of the things in life you are grateful for. This second journal keeps the positive energy flowing in your life and prevents you from slipping back into negative thinking and negative energy vibrations. The third journal is your "validation journal" and will be used for mirroring, acknowledging and loving your self. These journals are an important tool to "glue" and anchor you to your own life force energy and to establish a solid sense of your self. (Please refer to Part IV: "Exercises," for guidance in creating your "validation journal.")

Why Have You Forsaken Me?

Often during this incubation period where your boundaries are becoming firmer, you may feel jaded, you may feel resentful that the person you individuated from hurt you, and you may feel that your heart has shut down. You may feel let down by the greater powers that spiritually support you, and you may lose your faith in the Universe/God/Goddess/Higher Power.

It is okay to feel your anger, resentment, disappointment and pain. It is okay to feel sorrow for yourself. You need to experience these feelings before you can be a champion for yourself in the future and soothe and protect yourself from further harm. The act of self-love is the act of serving as your own protector, nurturer, and guardian. Before you can truly be there for yourself, you have to make sure you will never be a doormat again.

How then, do you learn to open your heart again? How do you learn to trust your own discernment about others' character? How do you trust others and let them in again?

Being Perpendicular

The answer is multi-faceted. It comes when you are able to stand firmly on your own grounding cord so that you do not need anyone else to make you whole or complete. You feel complete within yourself. Another will augment you instead of filling in any deficiencies and holes. If you did have holes, you would then be vulnerable to losing yourself within the relationship.

Picture two poles leaning on each other. If one pole leaves, the other one topples over and falls. Next, picture one perpendicular pole and one pole leaning on it. If the perpendicular pole leaves, the other pole topples and falls. Yet if the leaning pole leaves (usually due to death, because by definition, the leaning pole won't leave on his/her own accord due to dependency), then the perpendicular pole is still left standing. Finally, picture two perpendicular poles standing next to each other with a cord of love between them and connecting them. If one pole leaves (e.g. death), the other one is still standing, even though the severed heart cord causes mourning and grief.

"Leaning Position" versus "Perpendicularity"

If you truly allow yourself to go through the tunnel of angst and depression, and endure feeling the negative affect that ensues when you are individuating, then you will reclaim a piece of your soul that was frozen in past pain. You will be more whole and perpendicular by feeling the anxiety, depression and emptiness instead of defending against the fear of being alone.

If you truly have your self and you are perpendicular, you can risk entering another relationship, because no matter who abandons you, you will still have yourself to take care of you and nurture you. Hopefully, you will now have a discerning eye and sensitive radar, and you will be able to spot the energy/people who remind you of the people you were hurt by and from whom you have just extricated yourself. Then you can keep a solid boundary with these people so they won't be able to hurt you or unground you.

If you find yourself attracting another painful relationship into your life, then you have some frozen pain picture (i.e. experience) in your past that is acting like a magnet to attract this energy into your space. The energy is attracted into your space in order to "light up" the frozen past pain so that you can feel it and then remove it and heal it from your being. This process is done by individuating from that energy and becoming neutral to it.

If you find yourself mistrusting *everyone* and transferring old feelings onto safe and unsafe alike, then you will need to journey into a new layer of healing in order to open up your heart, to trust your ability to see clearly and to let in the "good."

How then, does one learn to let in and trust again?

Chapter 6
HEALING A HEART FILLED WITH DAGGERS:
LETTING IN THE "GOOD"

Let us use the following imagery to conceptualize the origins of how a heart shuts down or becomes broken-hearted in the first place. Imagine your heart center as a funnel of energy centered in your heart and radiating outwards. When you are born, your heart is completely open and you have the ability to give and receive 100% love. Next, suppose that an experience in your infancy hurt you and caused a dagger to be thrown into your heart (e.g. a parent punishing you, hitting you or yelling at you). You close your heart down a bit to wall off the dagger in order not to feel the pain inflicted by the dagger. Now your heart is about 95% open, and you can give and let in about 95% of the love. The 5% that is walled off harbors the dagger.

Then suppose another dagger was thrown into your heart. As an example, suppose for a parent or sibling made fun of you or rejected you. Your heart then shuts down another 5% to wall off the second dagger. Now you can give and receive only 90% love because the 10% comprising the daggers are walled off.

Over time, many more daggers get thrown into your heart. Your heart shuts down in order to wall off the painful segment where the daggers reside.

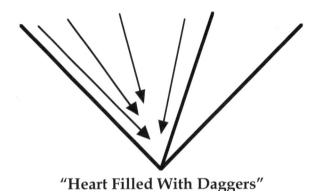

"Heart Filled With Daggers"

If you close the heart down, however, it keeps you from letting in and giving the life-sustaining energy of love. You unconsciously become a magnet for someone who is only capable of giving you the amount of love your heart has left open to receive. Therefore, if your heart is shut down, you will attract a person who is miserly or incapable of giving and receiving a lot of love. This person might actually throw the same kinds of daggers into your space that were thrown into your heart when you were younger. You may be blinded to the pain and so familiar with it, that you do not initially notice the pain. Interestingly, the word "familiar" comes from the root of "family."

As you individuate from the people who throw daggers into your heart, you begin to fill yourself with your own love. You may be able to extricate a few of the daggers through your own mourning and grieving during the therapy process and/or through meditation, and may begin to open your heart a bit more. However, the most painfully embedded daggers are the most difficult and frightening to extricate. Yet these deeply embedded daggers are the ones that need to be removed the most in order to have 100% of your heart's capacity again.

As your heart opens due to your own healing process and due to giving your own love back to your self, you will attract healthier people into your life, who have a greater capacity to love. This is where the healing process gets interesting.

Suppose a wonderful and benevolent person enters your life and gives you tenderness and love. In turn, suppose you decide not to be defended, and you are able to "let in" this love. It could cause you to cry or sob, because while it feels so good, it reminds you of what you did not get from the past relationships extending all the way back in your life. You begin to experience what you missed. If you feel the pain, a dagger can slowly be removed, as you let in the love in present time.

Let's also suppose that you have been betrayed, and that this betrayal dagger resides in the dark recesses of your heart space. You have a vigilant lens on your eyes as a result that does not allow you to trust. Next let's suppose that your "yes" category person gets a call for business and has to cancel your date. You immediately assume that he/she is betraying you with another person because you have been cheated on in the past, or because one of your parents cheated on the other. The next time you see this person, you will have the opportunity to either attempt to heal the dagger from the past or use your defenses to keep the dagger from reverberating. Hopefully, you can overcome the desire to defend yourself from the old hurt (e.g. shutting down, acting out by having a fling with someone else, breaking up etc.) and instead, you allow yourself to take the risk to be vulnerable. You may say something from a centered and neutral space, such as, "Your having to cancel our date brought back such painful memories and feelings because I have been cheated on in the past." The act of allowing yourself to be vulnerable by placing your heart out in the open to be healed, is crucial to the healing of the dagger.

The response you receive will be the true test to determine whether you are genuinely with a "yes" category, a "maybe," or a "no" category person. If the person understands your feelings and empathizes with your pain without getting defensive, then they are in the "yes" category. For instance, if he/she says, "Wow, how awful that must have felt for you," then just their understanding alone is enough to loosen the dagger from your heart. A series of these types of responses can actually extricate a dagger and help to build trust in your heart.

This is the type of healing experience psychologists call a "corrective emotional experience" (Miller, 1996). A positive response that is different from the expected, negative response serves to eventually desensitize the pain and replace the mistrust with trust.

However, if the person gets defensive by saying, "Why are you blaming me? I did nothing wrong," then the dagger will still be in your heart, and it will be difficult to trust when you are not being empathized with or understood. If this person is incapable of an empathic response, then you should protect your vulnerable heart and reconsider if this energy is healthy for you to be around.

In order to remove an old, painful dagger, it is usually required that a person understand, empathize with and love you. As the daggers are removed, you will be able to bring in the love where no love could gain access before. And you will be able to love yourself and be in affinity with yourself more fully and completely.

As you become more whole and perpendicular, you will attract healthier, more individuated people into your life. Like attracts like.

However, let's suppose you are still deficient in self-esteem, self-confidence and/or self-love. You will attract the energy into your life that frustrates these deficiencies until one of two processes occur. Either you will be able to fill the holes by yourself through loving and validating your self, or you will be able to leave unfulfilling relationships in search for more satisfying ones.

What do these unfulfilling and dissatisfying relationships feel like?

Chapter 7
ATTRACTION TO THE BAD

Burning Stoves and Dry Wells

An abusive, controlling or manipulative person can clearly be assigned to the "no" category. A person's abusive, controlling or manipulative behavior towards you can cave in your boundary and oppress you. Consequently, your spiritual freedom will be repressed.

I liken this type of person or energy to that of a "burning stove." You place your hand on the stove and it burns you. You tell yourself that the next time you make yourself vulnerable to this person, it will be different and you will not get burned. The next time you put your hand on the stove, however, it burns you again. You will continue to put your blistered hand on the stove and get burned until you finally reach the point where you say, "Ouch! My precious hand is being burned! I now know that I cannot change the stove, nor is the stove going to change." You will then decide to find a cooler surface on which to place your hand.

It is more difficult, however, to assign *nice* people to the "no" category. People who are incapable of giving to you what you need in the spiritual, emotional or physical realm may indeed, be wonderful people. Yet, if a large part of your self is not being fulfilled by the relationship, then you will feel "hungry," and you will not feel satiated in the partnership.

I liken this type of person or energy to that of a "dry well." You are thirsty and seek to quench your thirst to be understood, mirrored or accepted. You go to the dry well, hoping that it will quench your thirst. When the well does not offer you water, you feel frustrated, disappointed, angry or hurt. You tell yourself that next time, the well will be full and your thirst will be quenched. However, the next time you go to the well, it is dry and you become disappointed again. You will continue to go to the dry well and become disappointed until you finally reach the point where you say, "Argh! I feel so empty, unappreciated, disappointed and hurt. I now know that the well will always be dry." You will then decide to find a large, full well from which to quench your thirst.

There are two types of "dry wells." The first type is a person who may be in the "yes" category for many other people, but who is incapable of providing *you* with what you need. They may genuinely be kind and sweet, but they may not have the life experience, psycho-spiritual journeying, or emotional connection with themselves to be able to connect with you on a deeper emotional level. They may be smart, but they may lack the formal education you need to be able to connect with you on an intellectually stimulating plane. They may be sensitive and caring, but they may not be able to respond to your feelings in the way that makes you feel heard and understood. If this type of person is not able or willing to grow at the same rate you are, and if you are constantly feeling thirsty and empty, then you may need to move on, and seek a relationship that is more fulfilling for you.

For instance, one of my patients dated a wonderful man for five years. He had a doctorate degree in electrical engineering and was an analytical-type thinker. She was working on her doctorate in clinical psychology, and as she grew in the emotional realm from studying psychology and from being in therapy, she needed more emotional connection with her partner. Her partner strongly defended against experiencing his vulnerable feelings, and he could not connect with her on deep, feeling level. As much as she loved this man, she knew she needed a partner who was more capable of being vulnerable and who was more capable of connecting with her feelings and with her pain. She felt alone and disconnected from him, and she finally decided to make the decision, painful as it was, to move on and make herself available for a more fulfilling partnership in her future.

The second type of "dry well" is a person who consciously and intentionally withholds mirroring, acceptance and/or love from you in an attempt to hurt and frustrate you. This person may be passive-aggressive, competitive, narcissistic or sadistic. In all of these cases, you are made to feel invalidated, empty and longing for acknowledgement. You will finally reach the point where you are able to disconnect from the need to get acknowledgment or love from them when you allow yourself to feel the intense pain of the realization that your need will never be met by them. These thirsty feelings have to become so great and cause enough pain that it outweighs the desire to connect with the dry well. You will then be able to give love and acknowledgement to your self through self-validation.

Another patient's story illustrates this situation. This person was a beautiful, talented woman. Her mother was jealous and in competition with her for male attention, including from my patient's father, brother, and boyfriend. My patient longed for her mother to be supportive of her in her endeavors and loving towards her. The mother knew this, yet she consciously withheld any type of encouragement, mirroring, or validation from her daughter. Once my patient became aware of the dynamics and grieved because of the pain of not being able to receive the love she needed from her mother, she was able to let go and disconnect from the need. She was then able to bring into her life some "yes" category mentors who were positive, and who were not in competition with her. She was also able to learn to validate her self and give love to her self.

What developmental experiences create the need to be validated, mirrored or accepted? What causes the attraction to a "dry well?" The etiology of these needs arise from our infancy and childhood attachment to our primary caretaker. As we shall see in the next chapter, the attraction to "dry wells" is shaped by our early relationship experiences.

Chapter 8
THE ORIGIN OF LOW SELF-ESTEEM

The following chapter describes six roads that lead to the development of low self-esteem and the attraction to "dry wells." Theories from several schools of psychology are incorporated to illustrate the origin of low self-esteem.

Identity and Mirroring

As you may recall, the attraction to "dry wells" is shaped by our early relationship experiences. Based upon Heinz Kohut's work on Self Psychology (Baker & Baker, 1987), and Alice Miller's work on the ramification of having narcissistic parents (1981), some basic ideas on mirroring and empathic failures are explored.

During the "symbiosis" phase of early development, you feel "one" with your mother. You recognize her voice and know the taste of her milk. Hopefully, she will be "in tune" with your needs. If you are hungry, she will know this and will feed you. If you are wet, she will change your diapers. If you are lonely, she will pick you up, rock you or sing to you. You feel satiated and loved because your "thirst is quenched" and your needs are met.

During the differentiation phase, you begin to feel your body as separate from hers. You open your eyes and begin to focus. Hopefully, your mother will be reflecting "mirroring" responses back to you, and these mirroring responses help to shape your identity. For instance, if you are happy, you will gurgle and laugh, and you will be "mirrored" through her reflection back to you of your mood. She will make an animated, happy expression like you are making in order to reflect your happiness back to you. If you are upset, she will mirror a frown face and soothe you with her voice and cuddles. You know what you are feeling because your feelings are mirrored and reflected back to you. And you feel loved because your needs are responded to and your thirst is quenched.

Let's say, however, that mama is not in tune to you. Either she is overwhelmed with other crying babies, or she is anxious about not knowing what to do with you, or she is too self-focused, or she is resentful of you, etc. In any case, she is not there to change your diapers if you are wet, and she is not there to pick you up to soothe you if you are crying and scared. You will then imprint painful and hopeless memories of not being able to get your needs met. You will feel frustrated, angry or depressed. And you will feel empty and unloved (Baker & Baker, 1987). You may become so used to not being responded to that the emptiness inside becomes "normal" to you, and you will attract "empty wells" into your space, perpetuating deep thirst and emptiness.

When you become older, another part of your sense of lovability is formed. If your father (or mother) is mature and sensitive, you will feel seen and understood when you are with him or her. However, if he (or she) is narcissistic, you will feel like an object or extension of him/her, and will feel like you exist only if you are idealizing him/her and making him/her feel good and powerful. If he/she is immature, you will never feel like you are seen clearly because of his/her limitations and inability to relate to you. With a parent like this, you may become susceptible to attracting people into your space who need to be idealized and who do not see you clearly. Rather, they only see what you reflect about themselves back to them.

Alice Miller writes about the ramifications of having a narcissistic mother in her classic book, *The Drama of the Gifted Child*, (1981). She observes that children develop the "gift" of becoming numb to their own needs, and put their feelings aside in order to take care of the narcissistic parent's emotional needs. As a result, the child feels lost, with no sense of self, because in order to survive and receive love, she/he needs to tune into mother's needs and not tune in to her/his self. Consequently, she/he becomes susceptible to attracting the familiar "dry well" into her/his relationship space.

Anaclitic Depression

Feelings of despair, and the giving up of hope that anyone will actually pull through for you and "nourish" you, can sometimes be traced all the way back to the separation from a primary caretaker. This separation and loss occurs very early on during infancy.

In 1945, R.A. Spitz conducted a major psychological study examining what he referred to as "anaclitic depression," or a psychiatric syndrome of depression he observed in some of the infants in one group he studied (Pinneau, 1955). Spitz termed the syndrome "anaclitic depression" because he felt the clinical picture was similar to that found in depression in adults.

In one particular group in his study, pregnant, delinquent girls in a penal institution gave birth, and they cared for their infants until they were approximately one year old. However, a large proportion of the infants were separated from their mothers for three months, beginning at six to eight months of age. If the infants had to be separated from their mothers, the infants were cared for by other delinquent, pregnant girls, and were supervised by three assistants and a head nurse.

Some of the infants in the study developed the following symptoms: There was a drop in the developmental quotient, as measured by the Hetzer-Wolf baby tests; the infants were apprehensive, sad, and weepy, in contrast to their previously animated and extroverted behavior; they sat or lay with frozen, immobile faces and unblinking, expressionless eyes; they looked dazed, and appeared as if they were not aware of what was happening in their environment; and they engaged in self-stimulating, tactile behaviors.

All of the cases that manifested the syndrome of anaclitic depression had been separated from their mothers. However, not all of the cases that were separated from their mothers had developed the syndrome. Spitz concluded that the cause of the symptoms is the separation of the child from the mother (Pinneau, 1955).

Jenai Wu's (1997) article on anaclitic depression notes that if a person's issue with separation and loss has its roots in an anaclitic depression, the sadness in adulthood can be overwhelming, and the connection to life itself can be challenging. This type of despair can permeate one's relationships in the present, where it is felt that no one can nourish the soul's thirst, and the return to the "womb" or "tomb" or sleep is one's only solace.

Learned Helplessness

The feeling of having no control over one's physical environment can also be traced to experiences early on in life. Another significant psychological study conducted by Martin Seligman and Steven Maier (1967) studied the effects of "learned helplessness."

For their study, Seligman and Maier devised a shuttlebox for dogs. The shuttlebox had a floor that emitted electrical shocks. The dogs were placed in a harness in the shuttlebox room, and the experimenter administered inescapable shocks at random and varied intervals. The dogs soon learned that the termination of shocks occurred independently of their responses and of their attempts to escape the shock.

The dogs were then exposed to a new situation in the shuttlebox, where they could escape the shock by jumping a barrier. At this point, the dogs had given up hope that they could control their environment. They had actually "learned" their helplessness and no longer tried to escape the shocks.

Sad to say, humans can learn their helplessness too, if their control over their environment had been usurped early on. For example, suppose that a young child is supposed to telephone mother to pick her up when the ballet lesson or the Brownie troop meeting is over. If her mother is chronically late, the child will feel a sense of learned helplessness. In other words, regardless of whether the child calls or not, the mother is always late. The child may have difficulty believing that he/she could have any effect upon his/her environment, and is prone to feeling powerless and ineffectual later on in life.

Low Self-Esteem

Self-esteem is initially formed from receiving positive feedback and mirroring from another. Your "well" cannot be replenished by your self until you are "watered" by others.

Suppose, however, that your mother is unable to mirror you. Early on in life, your first "creation" is to make a "poopie." If she mirrors back disgust or disdain towards you or your "creation," you will internalize the negative reflection of your self and will feel bad, dirty, like a burden, or any other number of things depending upon her response. Later on in life, let's suppose that you bring home a finger-painting from pre-school. Based upon her response and reflection, you can have either a positive experience that builds positive esteem (e.g. she says, "What a lovely picture! Let's put it on the refrigerator"), or you can feel the narcissistic wounding of rejection, which leads to low self-esteem (e.g. she throws the picture away). Heinz Kohut notes that repeated empathic failures, rejections and harsh judgments will erode the esteem and confidence of a child (Baker & Baker, 1987).

Self-Consciousness

If one has been a victim of repeated judgments, rejections, criticisms, and/or jokes while growing up, then the experiences set this child up for becoming self-conscious or vigilant. I describe and conceptualize this state of being as a person having many "antennae" sprouting from on top of one's head. At the end of each antenna is an eyeball. These eyeballs scan the environment in a vigilant way to make the person feel safe. The eyeballs also look back upon the bearer, plaguing him with ruminating thoughts about what others think and feel about him.

The goal for these "alien-looking" victims is to pull their antennae back inside their bubble so that they can start viewing the world through their own eyes. In other words, instead of asking themselves, "What do they think about me?" they would ask, "Hmm, what do I think about them?"

If you find yourself becoming overly sensitive to people's expressions and/or comments, the antidote is to *seek clarification*. You need to be able to call people on the energy you are sensing from them so that you won't intuit in "overdrive" and become self-conscious. For example, if you sense a co-worker making fun of you behind your back, or if you sense him being upset with you, you can seek clarification by saying, "I sense some uncomfortable energy between us. Is there something you'd like to share with me?" If they validate your intuition and say, "Yes," then you have the opportunity to clear the air and get things out in the open. You would then know where you stand. If they deny the feelings that you are sensing, then at least you took control and activated yourself by asking rather than sitting with the uncomfortable feelings and thoughts that permeate your space.

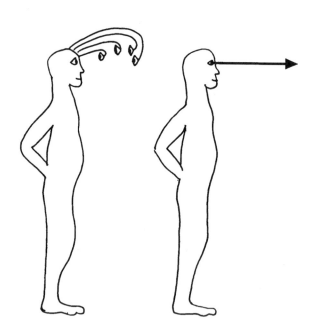

"Self-Consciousness" Versus "Assessment Made Through Your Own Eyes"

There is power in calling people on the energy that you sense they are projecting. "Seeing clearly" is a powerful tool to back down the energy of the offender. However, ignoring the energy keeps the offender in a position of power over you.

If the uncomfortable energy persists, your job is to figure out what percentage of the feelings are coming from past time and what percentage of the feelings are triggered from present-time reality. If, for example, you are feeling the same hurt feeling from your co-worker that you did at summer camp when you were a child, then go inside and look at the "picture" that is lit up in your space. Feel the original pain of being made fun of at summer camp. Allow your inner child to feel the pain. Then come back to present time. If you are able to make the connection between the present-time, co-worker trigger and your past-time, summer camp memory, then the uncomfortable, self-conscious feelings you have with your co-worker in present time will dramatically lessen. The self-conscious feelings will decrease because you realize that most of the "charge" from the picture came from your childhood past. The co-worker may still be a schmuck, and he/she may contribute to the percentage of the feeling being triggered, but if you are able to take most of the charge off of the trigger for yourself by bleeding the picture of past-time energy, then you will be much more comfortable, and you will be less "lit up."

If, however, you do not have any past pictures that are lit up in your space, but rather you sense the feeling is only coming from the present trigger, then trust your intuition about the ill feelings you sense from the co-worker, even if she denies any tension between you and her. Instead of feeling self-conscious, you can see the situation clearly and attribute the negative energy as emanating from her and not you.

In addition to seeking clarification, the other antidotal cornerstones for easing self-consciousness are self-soothing and self-validation. The more one learns to validate her self and love her self, the less one is concerned with how others view her. And the more one loves and embraces all aspects of her self, warts and all, the less judgment she casts upon others. If you point a finger at another, you will have three fingers pointing back at you.

Emptiness: Not Being Seen Clearly

Heinz Kohut notes that inaccurate mirroring can create a thirst for acknowledgment and approval from others (Baker & Baker, 1987). This thirst can sometimes feel insatiable. And a feeling of emptiness ensues when people do not understand you, see you clearly, or mirror your feelings accurately.

The key to healing this emptiness is three-fold. First, one must learn to validate and soothe oneself through such avenues as repeating affirmations, journal writing and meditating in order to find one's center.

Second, one must use her 6th chakra (i.e., inner eye) to "see" the reality that if people are not accurately mirroring you, it is because they are incapable of it. They may not be as far along as you are on the path of soul growth, and therefore, they cannot see ahead to the place where you are situated.

To conceptualize this point, imagine a baseline. Next, imagine a line vibrating five feet above the line. That is where the other person is vibrating. Then imagine a line vibrating ten feet above the baseline. This is where you are vibrating. The other person can see only the first five feet of your being because five feet is the limit of their vantage point. The other five feet of space above the original mark is invisible to them. Therefore they can mirror only a part of you that resonates with them but they will not be able to understand all of you.

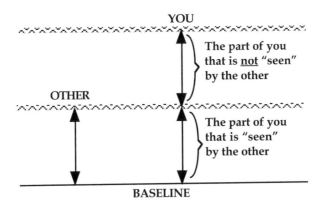

If a psychologically *mature* person does not understand or mirror you, it may be that the person has a picture or experience in his/her own space that prevents them from seeing you clearly. They may be in the "yes" category, but because they have not yet cleared the charge off of their *own* particular picture/issue that clashes with *your* picture/issue, they may not be able to see you clearly. A gentle confrontation stating your feelings, such as, "It hurt me when you did not understand what I was feeling," renders a heartfelt and apologetic response if the person is an old soul and in the "yes" category. For instance, they would respond with the statement, "I'm so sorry that I hurt your feelings." You will then feel seen and understood by the "yes" category response.

This fact leads to my third point, which is to then find old souls to flock with so that you will be seen fully and so that you will feel fulfilled. It may be extremely sad or painful to leave an empty well, but when a swan stops swimming with ducks and starts sailing with swans, the emptiness subsides and one feels full and alive.

The following case provides an extremely common example that illustrates how narcissistic wounding and empathic failures set the stage for unfulfilling relationships. One woman in my practice continued to attract noncommittal men into her life. She felt constantly rejected when the men could not love her in the way she longed to be loved. She never felt she was seen clearly or appreciated for the depth of her "being-ness."

Her father was a law professor. He was a "young soul," and was immature and narrow-minded. He was easily blinded by manipulating "no" category people, and was equally blinded to my patient's magnificence. He applauded and adored one sibling, who was mediocre at best, while he ignored the accomplishments of my patient achieved at her Ivy League graduate school.

My patient was in a lot of pain. Her defense was to control the situation by attempting to get her noncommittal partners to change and grow so that they would then be able to appreciate her. Her unconscious mind had attracted these "dry wells" and had set up the situations in an attempt to heal the pain caused by her father's limitations. If only she could get her partners to finally appreciate her, then she would heal her past pain through changing a young soul who was like her father. Sigmund Freud (1920) called this the "repetition compulsion," in which we are compelled to repeat the same patterns in attempt to change and heal the past (Gay, 1989).

In the beginning, she felt that the rejection was about her. Even though she was gorgeous, thin, a straight "A" student, and compassionate, she believed that if only she was "more perfect," then she would be loved by these men, and ultimately, she would be loved by her father.

Through the course of therapy, my patient began to feel anger and narcissistic rage about not being seen clearly and about not being appreciated or validated by these men. As she felt her anger, her self-esteem increased because she discovered that she was lovable and wonderful. Over time, she allowed herself to sink into the pain and submit to the truth. The truth was that she would never be loved by her father, not because she was unlovable, but because he could not do any better or be anything other than his limited self.

Once she accepted this painful fact, she was able to let go of her unfulfilling relationships. Once she did, she met a sweetheart-of-a-man whom she married. She gave up the struggle to be loved by her father and accepted him and where he was at in his psychological and spiritual development. She also was able to reach a level of compassion for his limitations.

Part II
DEVELOPING HEALTHY BOUNDARIES:
KEEPING OUT THE BAD - LETTING IN THE GOOD

Chapter 9
CATEGORIZING THE "NO'S","MAYBE'S", AND "YES'S"

As you are growing and journeying on your path, you will be individuating from "no" category people and weeding them out of your life, while bringing safer, benevolent, "yes" category people into your life. It is next to impossible, however, to eliminate all the "no" category people from your life unless you live in isolation. Some "no" category people may be family members, co-workers, neighbors or passerby's. And when you find yourself in their midst, you will need some tools and guidance to enable you to stay centered and neutral, and to enable you to become unaffected by their energy.

As you may recall, the "no" category person tries to control, manipulate, compete, sabotage and/or abuse you. The "no" category person may use abandonment, judgment, criticism, punishment, guilt, rejection, or any number of other energies in order to make you feel badly and in order to throw you off your center. Their intentions towards you are bad.

A "maybe" person is both malevolent and benevolent. He or she will switch back and forth between projecting good intentions towards you and then consciously or unconsciously hurting you.

The "yes" category person has nothing but good intentions and love for you. They feel safe to you. They are supportive of you without judging you and controlling you. Yet they are honest with their feelings, they are self-reflective, and they strive to be neutral.

To categorize your fellow planet mates into "no," "maybe" and "yes" categories, you must first make an *assessment* of their behavior from a space of neutrality. You must be in a neutral and present-time space in order to see with clear lenses. If you are not in a space of neutrality, but rather you are regressed and you are categorizing people based upon clouded lenses from the past, then you will be making a *judgment* and not an assessment. You will be projecting and transferring your feelings onto people, and you will be reacting to them from a non-centered position. The more you know yourself, the more you will know when you are regressed because experiences and emotions in a regressed state feel amplified, exaggerated and slightly surreal.

As you grow and individuate, however, you begin to accumulate experience and wisdom based upon previous encounters with "no" category energy. If someone in present time makes you feel similar to someone you had placed in the "no" category from before, and if you are in a neutral and present-time space, then you may trust your radar and your feelings. You must give yourself permission to see this person clearly instead of questioning yourself. It is often easy to override your radar and to tell yourself, "I must be neurotic or projecting because "so and so" seems to think this person is okay." It does not matter what others think. They may not have the same buttons or sensitivity to this person's energy as you do. Or, this person may treat them differently than they treat you.

The phenomenon of perception is fascinating. A person may be categorized as a "no" person by you, and yet the same person may be categorized as a "yes" person by another. This should not negate or invalidate your experience of this person. You may be a "no" category person to someone and a "yes" category person to someone else because each person has different issues and buttons that can be pushed. Every one of us experiences people differently.

What is critically important, however, is *your* experience of a person, and not others' experiences of a person. As long as you are in a reality-based space and not in a psychosis, you may trust your feelings.

Secondly, in order to categorize people into the "no," "maybe" and "yes" categories, you must trust what you see. Often, people invalidate themselves and minimize what they see about someone else's character and behavior because the ugly truth about another is too painful. Do not go into denial about what you see and do not make excuses for the person's behavior. Rather, file this persons' behavior in your memory. If the person shows no awareness about his offensive conduct and does not apologize from his heart, or if he continues to show the offensive conduct and bad character, then trust your perceptions about this person. If a person is usually benevolent and has a good character, but misbehaves or becomes hurtful on a particular occasion, file their hurtful behavior in your memory. However, you can forgive the behavior because it is out of character for this person. In other words, "file rather than go into denial," give a benevolent and self-aware, "yes" category person some slack, but do not let the unaware, malevolent, "no" category person off the hook. See him clearly and trust what you see.

Say, for example, that a blind person accidentally steps on your foot. The blind person was not acting from an ill-intentioned space and therefore, it is easy to pardon him because he did not mean you harm. If, however, a bully deliberately stomps on your foot, then you are allowed to feel your boundary being violated and you are allowed to feel the dignity emotion of anger. The difference between the blind man and the bully is their intent to harm you. Trust your feelings and file the behavior and the intent in your memory bank.

If you experience everyone as ill intentioned, however, you may be seeing through a warped, past-time lens, and you may be feeling through a charged, past-time picture. Again, it is up to you to know whether the emotions feel exaggerated and surreal, which is an indication that feelings are coming from a regressed space, or whether the feelings are indeed reality based. If you can separate the difference between the blind man's intention and the bully's intention, and if you can easily pardon the blind man, then you probably do not have an issue with being paranoid.

Third, based upon your assessment of this person's behavior and intent, decide whether this person is safe for you. Make the decision as to whether this person is worth knowing, pursuing, and connecting with. If your answer is "no," then give yourself permission to reject them. If they are rejecting or critical of you, then allow yourself the liberty of not having to get them to understand and accept you. If this person is abusive and/or addicted to drugs or alcohol, do not feel that you have to rescue them or heal them, because all they cause you is pain and suffering. They cause you to doubt yourself. You do not have to like everyone on the planet. Nor will everyone like you.

You do not have to feel guilty about placing a person into the "no" category. You can still be spiritual. You can still love this person from a "higher self" space, and you can wish this person no harm. But if this person is constantly throwing you off your center, and if this person makes you doubt yourself or caves in your boundary, then it is not necessary to like this person.

If your answer to the question as to whether this person is safe for you is, "Maybe," in that you see a glimpse of "yes" in this person but they are sometimes hurtful, then you can love the good parts about this person and decide to be acquaintances. However, you should not go into denial about his/her bad parts and become a victim to his/her stings. Nor do you have to waste your energy trying to change this person or make them enlightened and on your "path." Rather, accept them for where they are developmentally, and allow yourself to feel the pain of the realization that they are not aware and are not operating on the same level from which you are operating.

Due to the fact that a "maybe" category person is sometimes aware and sometimes unreflective and hurtful, you will be keeping a "maybe" category person at arm's length. You can open your heart to them when they are in a malevolent and good space, but you must be alert at all times because a maybe category person can sting you without warning.

If you categorize a person into the "yes" category, and if they are appreciative of your tender and precious heart, then it is okay to be willing to go through the effort to clear the air during difficult times. This is so because they have the capacity to connect with you and own their part in miscommunications. A "yes" category person is one you feel good to be around. They do not drain your energy field, nor do they invalidate you or throw you off your center. They can agree to disagree with you while also supporting you and validating your feelings. You are in your truth when you are with a "yes" category person.

How then, do you handle a "no" category person's energy if you are forced to interact with them? Since by definition, a "no" category person uses negative energy such as invalidation, criticism, judgment, punishment, abandonment, gossip, and so forth, to control you, and since "no" category people attempt to throw you off your center, it becomes imperative to keep your eyes open and to put your protective shield up when dealing with this type of person.

Chapter 10
TOOLS FOR "KEEPING OUT THE BAD"

The following section offers seven strategies for handling "no" category energy effectively. The first three strategies offer guidance for how to handle criticism effectively and the last four strategies offer guidance for how to set your boundaries. When these strategies are used, you will be equipped to maintain your center and to maintain your boundaries.

Don't Put Your Neck in the Guillotine

It is almost always desirable to express your feelings and confront an "offender" when they make disparaging remarks about you. If you do not confront the offender, you will be at risk of losing your boundary and "stuffing" your feelings.

However, do not allow yourself be vulnerable with persons you have categorized into the "no" or "maybe" category. If someone from these categories throws a "zing" at you and hurts you, do not expose your soft underbelly by choosing a verb that describes a vulnerable feeling when you confront the offender. In other words, do not say, "It *hurt* me when you . . . " because they will then say to themselves, "Good, now I know her Achilles heel," which will arm them to hurt you some more.

It is better to use a feeling word that appears as though it kept the zing from sticking to your soft underbelly. For instance, you might say, "It angered (or upset, or irritated, or aggravated) me when you . . . " Or, "I found you rude when . . . " Resist the urge to become reactive and defensive, and resist the urge to hurl a zing back to them. By doing so, you will sink to their level of negativity and will look and feel as badly about yourself as they do about you.

If you are with a "yes" category person however, you can share your vulnerability and say, "What you said really hurt me." If they are truly in the "yes" category, they will have compassion and love for you and will feel badly that you were hurt. They may say something in response, such as, "I am so sorry that I hurt you. That must feel awful for you." Due to the fact that their intent is to love you and not to hurt you, you will feel their compassion. Therefore, you will feel your heart opening up again after the slight has occurred.

Give Them Back Their Daggers

When someone overtly criticizes you, you want to say in effect, that you see their "daggers" clearly, and you want to hand them back their "daggers." If you do not call the person on their critical remark, you will run the risk of internalizing the criticism and will feel badly about yourself.

For example, one of my patient's "friends," who was a self-purported expert on everything, told my patient that my patient was "too intellectually beneath him to have a meaningful conversation with him." This person criticized my patient's intelligence despite the fact that my patient had a master's degree in philosophy and was quite well read in self-help psychology.

In response to this type of put down, you are encouraged to *describe* the dagger and *show the effect* the dagger had. To describe the dagger, you would begin your response with the statement, "I find your comment (insert adjective). For example, my patient could have said, "I find your comment disparaging," thus describing the criticism.

You would then show the effect the dagger had by adding the statement, "Instead of (insert 'doing' or 'being') _____ (insert adjective or phrase), you came across as _____ (insert adjective or phrase)." Thus, my patient might have added, "Instead of succeeding in doing what you intended to do, which was to put me down, you actually succeeded in having the opposite effect, which was to make yourself look supercilious and unbecoming."

Let's take another example of how to "give the 'no' person back his dagger." Suppose a person called you "fat." You would begin your response by labeling the dagger and you might say, "I find your comment to be critical." Then you would show the effect the dagger had and say something to the effect of, "Instead of being polite, you came across as mean-spirited."

These responses may take some time to construct, and you may not be able to eloquently address the daggers on the spot. In other words, you may find yourself having a delayed response to the criticism, and you may have to think about a response before you can confront the person. Over time, however, the responses will come quickly as you become able to stay centered and clear-headed when the attacks happen.

If you are not used to feeling the dignity emotion of anger, you may find that you don't even realize you have been insulted until much later after the insult has occurred. As you gain more awareness of when your boundary has been violated and as you get in touch with your dignity emotion of anger, however, an amazing thing starts to happen. The connection between the offender's insult and the feeling that was evoked by it will come closer together in time. Eventually, you will feel the insult occurring while it is happening to you. You will then be able to use your anger to activate your self so that you can confront the offender in a neutral and dignified manner.

Educating the Buffoon or the Jerk:
"Are You Aware That . . . ?"

Sometimes the criticisms and judgments from people are much more subtle than the overt criticisms that were previously illustrated. Often, the "no" category person's body language is critical, invalidating or judgmental, and it is easy to lose your certainty and question your feelings around this type of energy.

As an example, suppose you are working on self-esteem issues and have had parents or siblings who did not validate or mirror you very often. Let's also suppose that you find yourself feeling judged or criticized around these "no" category people because of the body language they exhibit towards you. You may be used to telling yourself that you are "just being overly sensitive" because you feel you need a lot of positive energy from people.

But who doesn't want to be around positive energy? Due to the fact that you are aware of your desire or issue to be mirrored and acknowledged, you may trust your radar, and you may validate the feeling that you are being criticized or judged. You will then need to pin down a specific comment or incident that would serve as evidence to back up your observation.

With the "no" category person, you are encouraged to call the person on the energy they are directing towards you. A good phrase to remember is the question, "Are you aware that . . .?" When you sense that someone's body language is ill intended, then interpret the body language and say something to the effect of, "Are you aware that you are coming across very judgmentally?" Or, you could say, "Are you aware that when you look away and roll your eyes, it comes across as if you are critical of me?" Or you could say, "Are you aware that when you use that tone of voice or when you sigh a lot, you come across as impatient?" Usually, calling a person on their energy stops them in their tracks because they are used to getting away with disparaging remarks. They are used to knocking you off your center and having power over you.

However, if you call the "no" person on the energy they direct towards you, they may fling another type of negative energy back at you. They may invalidate you by saying, "Oh, you are overly sensitive." Or, they may "gas-light" you (in reference to the movie classic, "Gaslight," where the husband's character attempts to make the wife believe she is going insane) by denying your reality and say, "I don't know what you're talking about. I never did that."

You are then encouraged to respond with a *neutral* comment such as, "How interesting that you see it that way." A neutral comment enables you to hold on to your perception about the interaction without losing your reality and caving in. It also keeps you on your center rather than on the defensive, as being defensive would end up making *you* look like the "problem child." The important thing to do is to call the person on their energy and make them aware that you are aware of their disparaging remarks.

Sometimes a "no" category person can surprise you and transform in front of your eyes. They may transform into a "maybe" category person who is possibly on the way to becoming a "yes" category person.

Suppose you take the risk to confront the "no" person and call her on her behavior. You might say, "Are you aware that you cut me off every time I start to talk about myself?" Given the opportunity, she might own the negative energy that she is directing towards you and reply, "You're right. I am harboring resentment over . . . " Or, she might say, "I do find myself getting impatient with you. What can we do about it?" If she is concerned about your feelings as well as her own, then she may be bumped up in the category scale. If, however, she defends herself and attacks you without acknowledging your feelings and allowing you your feelings, then she gets dumped back into the "no" category.

Setting a Boundary from the Neutral Zone

With respect to boundary setting, the single most important word you will ever learn to say is "no." It is your birthright to say "no." And it is possible to set a boundary without coming across as hard, unfeeling or angry.

Say for example, that you want to decline someone's invitation for a date. You need to state your boundary and say, "No thank you." You can also add the trailer, "but I appreciate your invitation," if you want to soften the statement.

If you are worried about the other person's reaction towards you when you set a boundary, you must remember that you are not responsible for their feelings. It is they who chose their response to your boundary setting. They can either chose to be respectful of your boundary by saying, "I understand," in which case they categorize themselves into the "yes" category. Or, they can throw "zings" and be partially defensive or punishing while also being understanding. For instance, they might respond, "Well, if you want to be a hermit, I understand," in which case, they would categorize themselves into the "maybe" category. Or lastly, they can invalidate you and try to make you lose your center by saying, "You are selfish," in which case they categorize themselves into the "no" category.

There is a way to deal with the "zings" without losing your center. You need to stay inside you bubble and imagine the energy that they throw at you as bouncing off of your bubble and away from you. This technique keeps you in the observing mode, where you can discern the specific type of energy that attempted to control you. This energy can be invalidation, judgment, criticism, punishment, abandonment, guilt, and so forth.

If you are not in the center of your head, but rather you are coming too much from your heart, then the "zings" can penetrate your bubble, hurt your feelings and throw you off your center. Being openhearted and innocent can blind you from the harmful energies in the early stages of boundary development.

It takes practice to be both in your head and heart simultaneously. Initially, when you are beginning to learn this technique, it is probably better to stay in your head in order to *observe* the energy, rather than to be in your heart, where you can lose your ability to see the negative energy clearly. Then, later, when your bubble is gelled so that it protects you, you can position your self in your head and heart space simultaneously without losing your self.

When the "no" category person has thrown negative energy at you for setting your boundary and saying, "no," allow the zing to bounce off your bubble and respond in a neutral way. When you are neutral, you are neither affected by their attempt to make you feel badly for setting your boundary, nor are you defensive.

To respond to the "no" person's "zing" in a neutral way, you will want to comment on their feeling without agreeing with their perception. A key phrase to remember for responding neutrally is, "How (insert adjective) that you feel that way." You can fill in the blank with any number of adjectives. In the above example, you may then respond to the disparaging "selfish" comment by saying, "How unfortunate that you feel that way." Or you could say, "How sad (or curious, peculiar, fascinating etc.) that you feel that way."

Don't Explain and Don't Defend

You do not want to explain or defend yourself when a "no" category person attempts to cave in your boundary. They can attempt to cave in your boundary by either trying to obligate you to do something you may not want to do, or they may cave in your boundary by criticizing, punishing, invalidating or judging you.

To reiterate, when dealing with a "no" category person, the best response is a neutral one, where you can agree to disagree. Sometimes the "no" category person may wish to engage you in an argument. If you bite, you will lose your boundary.

For example, let's suppose you are asked out on a date. You say, "No thank you," and they respond by saying, "You are selfish." You find yourself explaining yourself in attempt to make them understand you by saying, "No, I'm really not selfish. I am very sweet and give so much to everyone . . . " They can then refute you and argue with you until you give in or lose your center, or until you become upset because they don't believe you.

It is much better to simply say, "No thank you" and to resist the urge to explain your reasoning as to why you want to say "no." If you explain yourself to a "no" category person, they will refute your reasoning until you back down and give in to their request.

You will also lose your boundary with a "no" category person if you attempt to defend yourself. For instance, in the above example, they say you are "selfish" for declining a date. If you defend yourself and respond, "How can you say that? You don't even know me," then *you* look like the triggered one, and they can sit back and enjoy seeing your feathers ruffled.

It is much better to stay neutral, agree to disagree, allow them their opinion, and silently validate yourself. For instance, in this case you may say, "How unfortunate that you feel I am selfish," and leave it at that. Then quietly and internally validate yourself.

Often the "no" category people will fling a series of small but biting zings. It then becomes increasingly difficult to connect with them. Their zings are their protection and defense. You might deal with their zings by calling them on their remarks, using the "educating the buffoon" tool. Thus, you might say, "Are you aware that when you say such and such, you come across as being such and such?" Above all, with a "no" category person, remember the following mantra: "Don't explain and don't defend."

I'll Get Back to You

Sometimes "no" category people are neither attacking nor malevolent. Yet you feel either drained when you are around them or you feel pushed around by them because they are pushy and have no awareness or respect for people's boundaries. If either the "energy drainer" or the "pushy person" asks you to do something you'd rather not do, you can always respond with the phrase, "Let me think about it and I'll get back to you."

In the case of the energy drainer, suppose she catches you off guard and asks you to go on a short vacation with her. Let us suppose that you feel the need to get away on a vacation and think that it might be nice. The fact that she caught you off guard may make you susceptible to responding immediately to her invitation without thinking about the ramifications of spending a vacation with her.

In this type of situation, I encourage you to emblazon in your mind the response, "Let me think about it and I'll get back to you." This response neither obligates you to go on the trip, nor does it void the invitation. Instead, it will give you the time and space you require to make the decision from a centered space instead of from a harried space.

In another example, suppose a person is pushy and wants you to commit to something that you may not want to do. It could be a coworker or friend wanting you to baby-sit her five toddlers. It could be an acquaintance wanting you to be her maid of honor and wedding planner, or it could be something you really don't want to do, like training in the wee hours of the morning for a decathlon, even if by doing so, it would raise money for a charitable organization.

In all these examples, allow yourself some time to think about what it is you really want to do. You can memorize this phrase in order to have an automatic response, and tell them, "Let me think about it and I'll get back to you." Then you can prepare an appropriate response without obligating yourself.

Saying "No" to a Sweet Person

It is difficult to say "no" to a genuinely sweet person because you may feel guilty and badly if you hurt their feelings. It is important to be honest, however, and it is possible to be honest without incurring bad feelings and guilt.

For example, suppose a sweet colleague or friend invites you to lunch but you do not want to spend time with them. You can be honest and say, "I find myself feeling overextended and unable to put time into cultivating a relationship." You can also add a heartfelt compliment if you'd like, such as, "You seem like a sweet and caring person." You are being honest without necessarily damaging the person's self-esteem and heart.

If you acquiesce to the person's request and go out to lunch even though you don't want to, you will be compromising yourself and your boundary. And losing your boundary is the antithesis of being spiritually free.

A word of caution is appropriate. If you override your true feelings by sweeping them under the carpet, and if you acquiesce when you do not want to, the insidious energy of resentment will build in you. This resentment constructs a wall between you and the person you are interacting with.

Where does this resentment go? It will most likely turn inward, where you will stuff the emotion down with food, cigarettes, alcohol, or other types of anesthetics. Thus it is imperative to be honest with yourself and your feelings. The truth shall set you free.

Chapter 11
TOOLS FOR ACHIEVING A SPACE OF NEUTRALITY

The following chapter describes how to interact with others while being able to maintain a state of peace. You will be given three tools to assist you in maintaining a space of neutrality, and you will be introduced to three types of healthy communication processes to use in your interactions with others.

The ultimate goal for human beings is to exist in a space of "neutrality." What is meant by "being in a space of neutrality" is that you are neutral and non-reactive towards negative encounters. You are in "present time" and therefore, you are not regressed. The prerequisite for healthy communication is being in a neutral space.

When you are in a neutral space, you do not feel the intensity of emotions from your past that can get triggered as a result from interacting with others. Two pathways exist to enable you not to feel the intensity of these emotions. The first pathway is to feel your past pain and to "bleed" the emotional charge off past-time pain pictures in your space. You may have already had the experience in your life where you have healed a pain picture by journeying into your "well of pain" and have discovered that what once could hurt you so deeply, now does not bother you.

The second pathway for enabling you not to feel the intensity of emotions is to master the ability to "back burner" the regressed feelings that are triggered. In this way, you are able to stay in present time.

The goal in life is to become neutral to as many energies as possible. The more you grow and the more solid your core becomes, the less negative energy will affect you and "throw you off your center."

Grounding, Centering and the "Observing Mode"

There are three tools you can use to assist in achieving this space of neutrality and to enable you to stay in present time. They are the tools of "grounding," "centering" and being in the "observing mode."

You will be able to stay in present time when you use your bubble shield to protect you from becoming triggered and reactive. Visualize your self standing in the center of your bubble and behind your "shield." Next, situate your awareness behind your eyes. From this place, you are able to observe the world, rather than feeling that the world is observing you, and you will be in the "observing mode." From this "observing mode" place, you will be able to "see," discern and observe the type of energies whirling around and towards you, and you can shield yourself from these energies by having them bounce off of your bubble.

The "grounding" tool helps you to stay aware and awake in present time. The "grounding" tool prevents you from daydreaming or dissociating, which may blind you to other people's negative comments towards you. To ground yourself, imagine a cord that attaches the base of your spine to the center of the planet. When you use your grounding cord, you are reminded of your physical body in "present time."

The "centering" tool puts you in the "observing mode," where you can see energy clearly. To center yourself, imagine an energy cord extending from the heavens above. Imagine the energy flowing into the crown of your head and all the way down through your body and into your grounding cord. Next, center yourself on this axis of energy, and center your self behind your eyes. When you are situated on this axis, you are on the "observing mode deck."

When you are grounded, centered, and in the observing mode, you are healthfully detached from your thoughts and you are healthfully detached from your feelings. In other words, you observe your self thinking your thoughts and you observe your self feeling your feelings. You are therefore, able to *describe* to others how you are feeling from a "present time" and adult space.

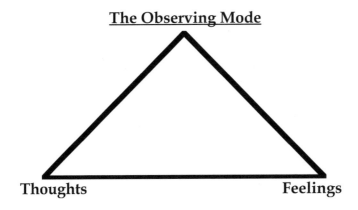

If you are disassociated and too disconnected and split off from your feelings, you will pontificate and intellectualize your feelings and become like Mr. Spock in Star Trek. If you are immersed in your feelings, you may become emotionally reactive and prone to act out your feelings. When you are in the observing mode, however, you will be in touch with your feelings, but you will be healthfully detached from them, so that you will be able to express your feelings in a neutral and dignified way, using "I messages."

"I" Messages Versus "You" Messages

The healthy and neutral way to communicate your feelings to others is from the first person perspective, using "I" messages. An "I" message is a statement that references you and your feelings. When you use "I" statements, you take ownership of your feelings and communicate them to the person with whom you are interacting. Examples of "I" messages are, "I feel hurt when you do or say (such and such) . . . " and "I feel angry when (such and such) happens."

In contrast, a "you" message is a blaming statement. A "you" message either blames the other person for making you feel a certain way, or it becomes a name-calling attack. For instance, in the above examples, a "you" message would be, "You make me angry when you do (such and such) and, "You are a jerk." If you use a "you" message, you will become reactive, and you will lose your space of neutrality.

The truth of the matter is that no one makes you feel a certain way. It is you who makes yourself feel a certain way because you ultimately have a choice over how you are going to feel.

Communicating your feelings from a neutral space means observing yourself experiencing the feelings and then communicating your feelings to the other person. For example, you might say, "I find myself feeling angry when you do that."

Your feelings are never right or wrong. They just are. You are entitled to your feelings, and hopefully, your feelings will be honored. People do not have to agree with your feelings, but they should respect your feelings and not judge, criticize or invalidate them.

When you communicate your feelings from an "I" message space, you are not putting people on the defensive, as you would be doing if you were to use a "you" message. With "I" messages, you are also giving people the opportunity to understand how you feel, coming from a neutral space. If people throw negative energy at you when you are expressing yourself from a neutral space, then their true colors are revealed, and they can be exiled from the "yes" category and dumped into the "no" category. A "yes" category person respects and honors your feelings.

The Tennis Court and the Weather Report

It is possible to have your feelings honored and respected without a person necessarily agreeing with your position. The goal of healthy communication should not be to sway a person's opinions and feelings in order to get them to agree with your position. Instead, healthy communication is about comprehending the other person's reality and having your reality understood.

Imagine a tennis court. You are on one side of the court and your friend is on the other. Your goal is to give your friend a "weather report" about the conditions on your side of the court and for you to hear and comprehend what the weather is like for your friend in the foreign land on the other side of the court.

To illustrate this point, you may say, "It's sunny and warm over here," and your friend may say, "Wow, it's cloudy and overcast over here." You might then respond, "I can understand how it could be cloudy and overcast in your neck of the woods given your location." You can experience an entirely different weather report and still understand and honor the other person's barometric conditions.

In turn, you can give your weather report, such as, "I felt really hurt when you canceled our lunch date at the last minute." Your "yes" category friend might then respond, "Wow, I can see how you would be hurt. From my side, I had no choice because my car broke down, but I can completely understand how you were feeling, as a result."

When you are giving a "weather report," you are expressing your feelings in a non-reactive way, and therefore, you are able to attain the peaceful space of neutrality. You will be acutely aware of the fact that you are dealing with a "no" category person if his part of the weather report is defensive and non-empathic. However, it feels like heaven when you are dealing with a "yes" category person, whose response is neutral, non-reactive and empathic.

Clearing the Static Off the Communication Cords

Healthy communication is also about "clearing the air" when tension and/or misunderstandings happen. As people become more aware of their feelings, and as they "move back into their bodies," it becomes increasingly more difficult to ignore energy and sweep feelings under the carpet.

Let's imagine that energy cords connect us to everyone else in our lives. If a misunderstanding occurs between you and another, there will be "static" on the cords connecting the two of you and you may feel a pang, flutter or twinge in your body. If you do not clear up the static energy and arrive at an understanding, the static will accumulate more energy, and before you know it, a barrier or wall can be felt between the two of you.

In dysfunctional families, it is status quo to sweep feelings under the carpet and never talk about what is truly going on. In these situations, the tension becomes so thick "you can cut it with a knife." If you come from this type of family structure, you will have to retrain yourself to *endure feeling the anxiety of confronting static*. For when you are able to do so, your connections will be clear and you will no longer feel isolated behind a barrier of stagnant energy.

It is common for people who come from families where communication patterns are dysfunctional to want to avoid confrontations at all costs. They like to keep the peace because clearing the static may cause uncomfortable feelings to emerge. If you don't take the risk to clear the air, however, walls will build. Connections will then seem superficial because the real feelings are not being addressed. If you take the risk and the other person reacts in a "no" category manner, then you don't necessarily want that person in your life anyway.

Chapter 12
SWINGING TO THE OTHER SIDE OF THE PENDULUM:
HAVING BOUNDARIES THAT ARE TOO BRITTLE

Once you have learned where your intolerance point exists and you have learned to establish your boundaries, you may be susceptible to forming boundaries that are too brittle. You may develop a low tolerance for any slight. This may be a temporary phase, or it could be the case of a deep-seated issue of narcissistic wounding that has finally emerged as your addictions, defense mechanisms and co-dependent "healing" behaviors have been transformed.

If, for instance, at this stage of the game, someone you have labeled in the "maybe" or "yes" category says something to you that inaccurately mirrors you and you feel hurt, slighted, insulted or misunderstood, then you may find yourself immediately shutting down your heart chakra towards that person and putting him/her into the "no" category. One needs to be cautious not to shut out people who do not necessarily need to be shut out.

Two steps need to take place. First, see the person's limitations clearly and have understanding, acceptance or compassion for *their* different lenses towards a situation. Secondly, move yourself into the observing mode, observe your hurt or angry feelings and soothe your self. Find any past-time hurts that were triggered, such as other times you felt misunderstood or hurt, and have compassion for your self and these hurts.

You may or not decide to process these feelings with the offender at that moment, but it is advisable to eventually clear the air and state your feelings if this person is important to you. Otherwise, the insidious wall of resentment will build and your heart will shut down.

It takes a certain level of maturity to be able to soothe your self when you are in pain. It also takes a certain level of maturity to communicate your feelings instead of shutting down and harboring the hurts and resentments.

If the person who hurt you has been in your "yes" or "maybe" category, the ultimate goal is to do your fifty percent of the process by opening up and sharing what is going on with you. If this person was in the "no" category, the ultimate goal is to soothe your self and process your feelings alone. You may decide to confront the "no" category person if you feel your boundaries were intentionally trodden upon, but the ultimate goal is to be able to see the person clearly and to be able to soothe your self.

It is up to the "offender" to do his/her fifty percent of the process by communicating his/her side to you. Suppose the offender does not communicate by apologizing or empathizing with your feelings while sharing his/her truth/feelings, but shuts you out instead. The bad feelings and negative energy will then be in his/her space and not yours, because you have done your part in clearing your side of the court.

If you shut your heart down *before* attempting to clear your fifty percent of the process by sharing your feelings about the interaction, then you are creating negative energy, which will result in blockages in your own energy field. You will also be squandering precious energy that will be required to keep negative feelings for that person inside of your own space.

You need to express your feelings, and you need to move the negative energy of hurt, resentment, or anger outside of your self and your space. If the feelings are not ameliorated by an apology or by an understanding response from the offender, then at least the negative energy is not residing in your space and festering, as you have attempted to move the negativity out of your space. It is then up to you to soothe your self and to have compassion for your self. In other words, have a "yes" category relationship with your self. (For practical guidance on soothing and validating yourself, please refer to the "Validation Journal" in Part Two of this book).

Ultimately, you will be centered and solid enough to "choose the timing of your battles." You will then be able to decide whether and when to respond to a zing and slight and when to internally soothe your self and let the zings and slights go for the moment.

For instance, suppose the person who is offending you is in a bad space and you have enough awareness and compassion for this person to recognize their regression. You may then decide to take the higher road of compassion and decide not to respond immediately to the offense. However, after the person has come back to her/his center, it is advisable to say something about your feelings so that the insidious wall of resentment does not build.

Chapter 13

PARTNERSHIPS

It is often said that relationships are the ultimate test. Everything you have learned about communication and boundaries gets tested when you are in a partnership that is close to your heart.

Old issues are more susceptible to becoming triggered when we are in partnerships. As we let in intimacy, our vulnerability to rejection, abandonment, loss of identity and self-esteem is heightened and "on the line." While the following discussion can apply to any interaction you may have, the emphasis on partnerships puts the focus on the patterns of interaction that you may have with a person who is close and meaningful to you.

The Child, Adult, and Parent Within

I do a lot of work with couples. Frequently, one partner may feel hurt and misunderstood by the other partner at any given time, even when both partners have categorized each other into the "maybe" or "yes" categories. If at least one person is centered when a slight occurs, then it is possible for an understanding to occur between the couple.

For instance, suppose the person who said something to offend the other person is centered, and the "victim" becomes hurt and regresses into a pain picture from the past. The centered "offender" can then respond in a "yes" category fashion and apologize to, or soothe, the regressed victim. On the other hand, suppose the "offender" is regressed and says something to the "victim," who is in a centered position. The centered victim will then be able to see the regressed place that the offender is in and will be able to internally soothe him/herself until the regressed "offender" returns to a centered position.

The problem occurs when both partners are regressed simultaneously. If both are feeling hurt, and if both are regressed into past-time pain pictures, they will not be available in present time to deal with either their own hurt or their partner's. Each will likely push for the other to heal their own respective pain pictures, and each will want the other to understand the pain they are experiencing. When the psychological resources are not available for each to do so, defenses can go up and hearts can shut down.

We each have three modes of personality within us: a child, an adult and a parent (Berne, 1958). The "child" is the place to which we regress when we are triggered by an encounter and we feel our past-time pain. This is because our inner child has been hurt, and we feel the hurt like we did when we were little.

The adult persona is our mature perspective. We are in "present time" when we are in the adult mode. We can see any given situation through mature lenses, and we are "centered," rational and grown up when we are coming from our adult perspective.

In our parent persona, we act from a "rule oriented" and critical perspective. We feel like "the authorities," as we may have viewed our parents, the police or schoolteachers when we were growing up.

Both the child perspective and the parent perspective are regressed spaces. Both of these perspectives cloud your lenses, precluding your ability to be mature, centered, in present time, and in a space of love and compassion.

Eric Berne (1958) used the term "transactional analysis" to address the child, adult and parent levels of interactions that can occur between people. There are three levels you may be coming from at any given time, and three levels that your partner or others may be coming from. The six combinations of interactions make up what is a useful grid for analyzing communication patterns between two people.

Adult-to-adult communication occurs when we are in our adult perspective and others are in their adult perspectives. We have present-time communication that is untainted by past baggage that we may be carrying. Communication feels healthy, which is why adult-to-adult communication is the ultimate goal for relating with your partner and with others in general.

Child-to-child communication occurs when you are in a regressed child space and your partner is also in a regressed child space. If you are operating from your child perspective, and you are regressed into a hurt or angry feeling that you experienced as a child, you may be seeking the soothing, nurturing and understanding that you longed for from your parent. If your partner is operating from his/her child perspective, however, you will not get the nurturing you crave because your partner is also regressed, devoid of resources, and perhaps is pulling for you to be adult and nurturing. This "child-to-child" interaction is difficult to resolve in the moment because both of you are regressed. You will have to wait until both of you return to a centered space in order for each to be able to give what the other needs.

Child-to-adult interactions occur when one partner is regressed and the other partner is in present time. If you are regressed, and if your partner is in the adult mode, then hopefully, your partner will be able to see your "inner child" and have compassion for your pain while you are feeling and living in a past-time place. If your partner is regressed, and if you are in your present time, adult space, then you will have the resources available to have compassion for your partner's pain. When this is the case, you will not react defensively while your partner is in his/her child space.

If either one of you is resistant to feeling compassion towards the other when he or she is regressed into the child mode, one of three scenarios may be unfolding. In the first two, part of you resists being compassionate due to a trigger within that clashes with your partner's desire for nurturing and understanding. In this case, you are likely coming from your critical, judgmental or authoritative parent space. Or, you may be coming from your inner child space. In the third scenario, you are in your adult space, yet you may have become impatient with the frequency and duration of your partner's regressions. You may feel compassion for you partner's pain and be able to speak to it, but you also long for your partner to return to his/her center.

Child-to-parent interactions occur when one partner is regressed in the child space and the other partner is regressed in the critical or authoritative space of a parent. If you are in a regressed space and your partner is in his/her parent space, then you may feel hurt and angry while your partner reacts in a harsh, critical or judgmental way. Likewise, suppose you are being critical, judgmental, or behaving in a controlling and authoritative manner, and your partner is regressed into his/her childhood pain. Neither the child pieces of the dyad nor the parent pieces of the two of you can be appeased in the moment until either the "child" soothes him/herself and returns to one's center, or the "parent" mellows out and recognizes his/her own negative behavior. In these scenarios, a period of "time out" may be called for in order for both parties to return to their centers.

In the adult-to-parent interaction, one partner is centered while the other is behaving in a controlling, authoritative, critical, condescending or harsh manner. Suppose the centered partner stays in a space of neutrality and does not react in a defensive manner towards the partner's destructive behavior. Nor does the centered partner regress into a child space, where her/his boundaries can be trampled upon. The negative behavior will then boomerang back onto the "parent-spaced" partner, nudging this partner to have a look at his or her own behavior. In this instance, the centered partner's neutrality will have served as a mirror that reflected the negative behavior back to the partner.

Parent-to-parent interactions create a real power struggle because both partners try to control and coerce the other into submission. These interactions feel ill intentioned, abusive, manipulative, critical and condescending. Both partners feel righteous and "lock horns," so to speak. If both partners had instead been in an adult space, each would have remained in neutral territory. Each would feel certainty about his or her own feelings. Each would also be respectful of the other's feelings.

Suppose a person's child or parent persona becomes entrenched and problematic, in that they have difficulty returning to their center. Therapy can then help a person work through the pictures/issues that taint the individual's ability to have present-time communication. If one partner seems predominantly regressed in his/her child or parent space, and if he/she rarely has present-time and neurotic-free communication with the other partner, then individual therapy is usually preferred to couple's therapy. The goal of individual therapy is for the pictures to be worked through sufficiently to enable this partner to develop an anchor that will position them in the adult perspective.

It is an ongoing challenge to anchor your self in present-time adult, mature and compassionate space. Nevertheless, when you make the decision to live life consciously, and when you observe yourself in "action" rather than live in "reaction," your life will become more peaceful. Moreover, the people around you will be attracted to your grounded and positive energy.

Communication Patterns in Action

The following examples illustrate various communication patterns common to couples I see in therapy. While the cases present one of the partners in a child space and one of the partners in the parent space or adult space, none of the spaces is more common to a particular gender, as both males and females are equally likely to assume any of the roles illustrated.

The first case illustrates a situation where one partner was entrenched in her child space and was unable to move into her adult space until she received the reassurance and trust that had been destroyed as a child. The other partner was in an adult space and able to heal her pain.

She was a social worker, and her first marriage ended in divorce after her husband had an affair. Her father had cheated on her mother and consequently, she had lost her trust and faith in men.

He was a veterinarian. He became a widower, following the long illness and death of his wife. He was a warm-hearted and becoming gentleman who had lost both parents at an early age. Consequently, he possessed some fear and pain around the issue of abandonment.

During the first year of their relationship, they came to see me because she was fearful that he was cheating on her. It was necessary for him to leave early while they were on dates, or to cancel the dates all together, when emergencies would arise at his clinic. She was convinced that he was lying to her, and he was stymied as to what to do about it. He would explain the facts surrounding the situation from a rational and somewhat detached space. At times he would get frustrated at being falsely accused.

She was regressed in her child space and could not hear the facts about him having to take care of the animals at the clinic from an adult, centered space. What she needed from him was warm-hearted, soothing and compassionate reassurance that would speak to her frightened, inner child.

Once he recognized that this beautiful, grown woman was actually a hurt and scared thirteen year old, he chuckled, and was able to open his heart to her pain. He did not become defensive or behave in a judgmental manner. Rather, his inner nurturer emerged. He was able to stay in his adult space and soothe her frightened and mistrustful inner child. He actually felt relieved and reassured to know that she cared so much about him and would never leave him.

The story does not end here, however. While his repeated responses helped to open her heart somewhat, she continued to have issues concerning mistrust. She could not remain in her adult, centered space for long, and she continued to be hurt, angry and untrusting.

Upon further analysis, a few additional details needed to be sorted through. He was a friendly and well-liked man. Women often would talk with him in her presence and some would even flirt. He, being somewhat naive to the overtures of women, would continue to be friendly towards them. He was unable to pick up on the subtleties of their overtures. This behavior by women towards him filled my female client with insecurity. When she confronted him, however, he would become defensive, stating that he was doing nothing wrong by being friendly.

I then informed him with respect to the issues of "female competition." I let him know that some women love to flirt with other women's partners as a way to punish the "competition" and to feel powerful. He had no idea that some women would actually try to hurt his beautiful partner by stealing him away. Once he became aware of this, he no longer acted defensively. Instead, he acted protective towards his partner, and he became formal instead of being overly friendly towards women when they would flirt with him. Moreover, any time women began to flirt, he would put his arm around his partner to make it clear that he was with her.

Due to his capacity to stay in his adult space and reassure her inner child, she slowly but steadily established trust and security in the relationship. She was then able to stay in her adult, present-time space. She was able to separate the childhood feelings she had been transferring onto her partner from present-time feelings that she had for him. Consequently, communication channels opened on a healthy, adult-to-adult level.

It should be noted that my female client had been psychologically ready to have her childhood pain "light up" so that it could be felt and cleared away. Finally, she had unconsciously chosen a safe man who would not cheat on her. Thus, her insecurities were able to come to the fore in a safe environment, where they could be released as she opened her heart to him. The alternative would have been for her to continue to defend against feeling betrayal pain by keeping her heart closed in unsafe relationships. But she was ready to open her heart, ready to feel the pain and to move through it in order to extricate the "daggers" that had been embedded during the past. While the process wasn't easy, she ultimately healed herself of past wounds by entering into a good and solid relationship.

The next case illustrates the dynamic of a child-to-parent interaction. During the course of therapy, the dynamic moved from a child-to-parent interaction to an adult-to-parent interaction and finally, to an adult-to-adult interaction.

He was a contractor and owner of his own home building company. His father had been in the military and his mother a homemaker. His father had been very strict with my client, and pushed him to excel in sports and other endeavors by adopting a militaristic and critical approach to "challenge" my patient. Thus my client became used to using harsh, negative reinforcement to motivate himself and others instead of being positive and supportive towards them.

She was a second grade school teacher and the youngest daughter in her family. Her father had been an attorney, and was very judgmental and analytical. She was her father's "favorite," partly because she idealized her father and never challenged him on his critical and judgmental approach to life. As long as she stayed in a subservient role and acquiesced to her father, she was "loved" by him.

This couple had been married for seven years. They entered therapy because they were beginning to fight frequently, and had arrived at an impasse. In the beginning of their marriage, she had idealized her husband, and enjoyed his role as the "man of the house." As time passed, however, she began to feel criticized and devalued, and finally became depressed.

When, for example, they would have discussions about local news events or philosophical ideas, she would state her opinions and he would immediately bat them down. She would regress into a "hurt child" mode and experience feelings she had not allowed herself to feel in her relationship with her father as a child. She had idealized him and repressed those feelings back then. The idealization had been a defense mechanism against the fear of challenging her father and creating a conflict. As she grew in her career, however, she began to speak her mind more often, and when this carried over into her marriage, the conflicts began to occur.

My male client was used to having his opinions be the only opinions aired and could not see why his wife was upset and hurt. When she would cry in response to his taking a stand and disagreeing with her, he felt she was overreacting. On her side, she felt invalidated that he treated her like a child who should "be seen and not heard."

This stage in their relationship illustrates a classical parent-to-child interaction, where both parties are regressed in past-time feelings and are not connecting with each other. He was coming from his parent perspective, which was harsh, authoritative and critical. She was coming from her child perspective, which was hurt and ineffectual.

As the therapy progressed, however, she came in touch with her anger and hurt towards her father for making her feel "like a pretty face with no brain." Then she was able to own the responsibility for allowing this feeling to happen. She had repressed her feelings because she did not want to create conflict and lose her father's love. As she moved through the fear of losing love if she spoke her mind, and as she separated from the energy that controlled her, she was able to move herself into the present-time, adult stance and talk about her opinions with her husband.

Initially, this change in her created friction between the couple, as the husband could not grasp the concept that two people can "agree to disagree." He had difficulty comprehending that both party's opinions can be valued and respected in any philosophical debate. The wife was able to grasp this concept, however. She learned to become neutral to her husband's harsh and controlling energy by not reacting, arguing or regressing, while continuing to maintain her position on a point.

At this stage in the dynamics, the interaction was adult-to-parent. The wife had moved from her child perspective, where she would regress and get upset, into the adult perspective of neutrality. She was able to state her opinion and not lose her certainty while allowing her husband his perspective, even though he remained obstinate in his opinions.

This position of neutrality had a powerful effect on the husband's regressed, parent persona. The act of remaining neutral and of not reacting to a person's defensive position causes a boomerang effect. The person's defense pounces back to them. So by taking the adult stance, the wife brought to light the husband's regressed, obstinate conduct, and he recognized his behavior for the first time. With no place for it to go, it boomeranged back to him. He then understood how awful it was to exert this type of power over someone. He was able to see how he had identified with his father, and he recognized that he had assumed his father's role in order to avoid feeling powerless. At last, the husband was able to get in touch with his buried childhood pain and to feel the hurt and anger caused by not being treated by his father with support and love.

At this point, the dynamics moved into an adult-to-adult relationship. From his adult perspective, he was able to be more authentic and caring. No longer did he have to defend against feeling his childhood helplessness by playing the role of a harsh and powerful parent. She was able to be more assured and confident, and no longer had to defend against the fear of losing love because she challenged authority and stated her opinions. The two of them were both able to connect with each other in "present time." They now have an ongoing, healthy marriage.

The next case illustrates the dynamic of a child-to-child interaction. During the course of therapy, this returned to an adult-to-adult dynamic.

This couple had been married for two years. She was a professor at a major university and held a doctorate degree. He was a CEO of a dot.com firm. Her mother had recently passed away. The mother had been extremely withholding towards my patient, both in terms of love and acknowledgment. She favored my patient's sister over my patient, and my patient never felt that she was understood, acknowledged or important.

He came from a close-knit family, but his family did not communicate feelings towards each other. Instead, they ridiculed and jibed each other. This made him sensitive to criticism.

Both partners were quite intelligent, psychologically aware, and each had a capacity to communicate with the other from their adult personae most of the time. Problems arose, however, when my female patient felt as though he did not care about her, or that she was not important to him. He in turn felt criticized. These situations occurred when he was too tired to do the extra little things she longed for, such as organizing weekend getaways on his own accord or leaving her loving messages on her voice mail. She would then feel unimportant and unappreciated.

She would experience the pain of her childhood, and want him to respond by "doing things better." She wished for him to be in tune to her needs and did not want to have to spell things out for him. She said that she would feel loved and important "if only he would tune in to what would make her happy." Her child space was triggered, and she experienced the same feeling of being unimportant that she had felt as the result of her mother's treatment of her.

He, on the other hand, would feel censured for the things he did do for her, such as planning baseball outings and washing the cars. From his perspective, what he did for her never seemed to hit the mark. As a result, he felt his childhood pain of being criticized.

He would become defensive and attempt to explain himself when she was regressed in her child space. During these times, she experienced the pain of being unimportant and of not being empathized with. She would react to his defense of himself by criticizing his "half-witted efforts" to do the things that would make her happy. He would then regress into his child space of feeling criticized no matter what he tried to do. This made him feel like doing nothing at all.

The child-to-child communication pattern would then be established, where neither partner could console the other in the moment. It was difficult for either to return to their center with respect to the interaction because each person's childhood pain was triggered, and each needed the other to behave differently in order for the problem to go away. She wanted him to intuitively know and do what she felt were the perfect loving things, and he wanted her to be less critical of the things he did, even if they were "off the mark."

During the course of our work together, each partner learned to get in touch with the origin of their pain, the trigger so to speak, and to soothe and validate themselves instead of expecting this from the other. They learned to share the source of their triggers so that each would have compassion concerning what set off the other. Each learned to do this while sharing and receiving the information from a centered and neutral space.

In a couple relationship, if the child in your partner is unable to speak to *your* inner child, you must stay in your observing mode and recognize that the other person is regressed and unable to mirror you. You must also soothe your own inner child. You must summon your own nurturing parent within to give your inner child what he or she needs. Then you can keep your heart open towards your partner.

For instance, she was able to experience the pain of feeling that she was unimportant to her mother. She was able to soothe her self and grieve for herself over this pain, and she was able to share the pain with her husband from her centered, adult space. He was able to recognize her pain after she moved from her angry/hurt child space to her centered and neutral adult space. He was able to understand her pain from his adult space without feeling criticized because he could see where her pain came from in her childhood. He could separate her childhood feelings from his own childhood trigger, thus realizing that he was not incompetent or "half-witted."

In addition, he was able to get in touch with the childhood pain he possessed of being chastised and criticized. He learned to validate in himself what he did for her, and he was able to share his childhood pain of feeling criticized from a neutral and centered space. She could see his pain with her heart from her nurturing space, once he was able to move from a defensive and angry child position to his neutral adult space. She was then able to let in the energy of love generated by the things he did for her, even though they were not the things she had in mind. She was able to feel the "thought behind his gifts" to her.

Because each of the partners had the inner resources to move themselves into their adult space, they did not need to try to elicit soothing and validation from each other. They had enough ego strength to soothe their own inner children and consequently, both were able to find their adult spaces that pertained to the issues that clashed.

Negotiating Space and Boundaries in Relationships

A common occurrence that I witness between couples is that of negotiating "alone time" versus "togetherness time." Usually one partner wants more togetherness time. When this partner begins to feel their child space feelings of abandonment, he or she will become "clingy" in the relationship. The other partner may prefer more alone time. When their partner starts to cling, they will feel their child space feelings of engulfment and become aloof as a result.

When one realizes that these abandonment versus engulfment feelings stem from the child space within, it becomes easier to soothe one's self or to have compassion for one's own feelings and the feelings of one's partner. In other words, armed with understanding, it is easier to refrain from reacting and taking personally the partner's feelings. It is also easier to negotiate boundaries regarding "alone time" versus "togetherness time" time from the centered, adult space.

I find it interesting that there appears to be a direct relationship between one partner's feelings of abandonment and the other's feeling of engulfment. If one partner is aloof and has engulfment issues, the other will experience abandonment feelings more intensely, and will perhaps become "clingy." Yet if this same "clingy" person is later with an engulfing partner, the new situation will bring out this individual's engulfed feelings, causing the person to become more distant and aloof.

We all have engulfment and abandonment issues because we all went through the individuation process from our primary caretaker early in our lives as infants and toddlers. Some of us went through the individuation process more successfully than others, and can therefore tolerate the negative affect of abandonment (e.g., being alone) or engulfment (e.g., being close without losing your sense of self) more easily than others. Nevertheless, the tether between these two states resides within all of us.

Negotiating "space" boundaries from a centered, adult space can help ease tension that may otherwise occur between couples. The ideal situation is for partners to discuss their desires for together time and alone time from an adult perspective. These times can be scheduled. Moreover, each should have a mutually-agreed-upon place within the home where they can be alone. This will prevent engulfment and abandonment issues from being triggered.

The following case involves a couple for whom childhood issues of abandonment versus engulfment were problematic. He was an architect and she was an interior designer.

When these partners initially got together, they wanted to be together all the time. They spent weeknights and weekends in bliss. After about three weeks, however, she felt burned out and needed some time away from her partner. She wanted to be alone and also to spend some time with her girlfriends. He felt abandoned and as a result became insecure and clingy. She reacted by becoming irritable and moody. She fantasized about breaking up with him because she felt so engulfed. Yet she did not want to be completely alone.

Whenever she would try to take off a night or two from seeing him, he would regress into his child space, feel abandoned and get upset. She would give in and see him, but would feel angry and moody as a result.

It was interesting to learn that in each of these partner's prior relationships, the roles had been reversed. In his past relationship, he was the "distancer" who felt engulfed. In her past relationship, she was the one who felt abandoned and had been "clingy." Her previous partner had been emotionally aloof.

I explained that an abandonment versus engulfment tether resides in all of us. He was able to use his past relationship as a bridge to understanding how she could be feeling engulfed. After all, he had felt the same way in his past. Likewise, she was able to understand the intense abandonment he felt once she recalled how she had felt in her prior relationship.

The couple worked on how to gently negotiate space boundaries while having compassion for each other's inner child. For instance, she learned to set her boundaries with tenderness and speak to his child space feelings when she needed time alone, instead of abruptly reacting from her engulfed child space by being cold and defensive. She would first reassure him that she loved him and wanted to be with him and then express that she needed to recharge herself so she would be all the more present and attentive when she returned. He was able to express how much he would miss her, and to tell her that he loved her and wanted to give her the space to recharge. He was able to tolerate the temporary disconnect and soothe his own inner child instead of becoming upset and acting out his inner child.

The couple was able to negotiate in advance which days would be spent together and which days would be spent apart. Knowing in advance when they would be together and when they would be apart helped each to be prepared when regressed feelings were triggered. When she felt engulfed, she would know that she would soon have time alone. When he felt abandoned, he would know that he would be getting together with her soon. As time passed, the trust and love between this couple grew strong and the regressed feelings began to subside. Later, the couple were married.

The Healthy Communication Pattern

To insure healthy communication one needs to operate from their adult space and speak from a centered and present-time position. In this way they will not be reacting from regressed, past-time feelings. If old feelings are triggered, a person needs to be able to get in touch with these feelings, move back to present time, where they can, from a neutral position, communicate what they feel to their partner.

Let's say that your partner is in the "yes" category, but says something that hurts you. The process should begin by allowing yourself to get in touch with your old hurts or "pictures" that were triggered. The "charge" or pain from these pictures is coming primarily from the past. Once triggered, you are ready to feel the pain and discharge it. You will experience the pain and soothe your self, and then come back into present time. If you have done the healing work around a particular button, this process can be almost instantaneous, or it can take longer if you need some time to analyze the pain. If you can feel the initial wounding from the past, then you will be able to bleed off most of the charge from the pain picture, since most of the pain was coming from the past and not from the present.

The balance of the pain caused by the trigger is from real or present time. It is up to you to communicate this. Clear the air by mentioning your feelings to the offender (i.e., your fifty percent).

Your "yes" category partner, by definition, will then apologize or explain his/her side and have compassion for your hurt (i.e., their fifty percent). If your partner has been compassionate about your pain and has apologized from his/her heart for the pain he/she caused, then it is should be easy to forgive the offense and let go of the feelings. Your heart should feel open because you have expressed your feelings, your feelings have been embraced and understood, and you feel connected with your partner.

Let's back up to the point where your "yes" category partner gives you a heartfelt apology. What happens if you still feel hurt and you find your heart shutting down. Even though he/she has understood your pain and apologized to you, you may find yourself still resenting your partner for hurting you. How does one reach the space of acceptance, compassion and forgiveness? This will be addressed in Chapter 14.

Chapter 14
FORGIVENESS IN PARTNERSHIPS

Two obstacles, or regressed spaces, prevent or hinder forgiveness in partnerships. One is when the partner becomes entrenched in a "parent mode" space, and the other is when entrenched in a "child mode" space. A person is best able to forgive when in the centered, mature space of the "adult mode."

Having Compassion for Yourself and Others

If you find yourself resenting your apologetic "yes" partner for hurting you, it may be because you are coming from your righteous, parent space, and you are judging the offender for his bad behavior. At this point you may need to take a look at your own behavior.

If we judge others for their mistakes and misguided behavior and hold a grudge even after they apologize, we should examine the part of our selves that is capable of doing the same thing they did to us. Almost always, when you have one finger pointing at someone, three fingers will be pointing back at you. It is impossible to forgive others before we have forgiven our selves. Moreover, having compassion for your self when you have made mistakes can lead to having compassion for others when they do the same.

Once you have compassion for your self, you can *understand* how the other person could say or behave in a particular way. You may not like the behavior or agree with it, but if you reflect on times when you have also made mistakes and said things you regret, then it will be easy to have understanding and compassion for the offender.

This is not the same as going into the "understanding mode." As you may recall, the "understanding mode" is the defense mechanism that keeps you from feeling your own anger/dignity emotion when your boundaries are trodden upon. In the previous example, you are not sweeping your feelings under the carpet, as you would be in the "understanding mode," because you vocalized your feelings and set your boundary when you felt hurt.

If you have ever unintentionally hurt someone and found that they held a grudge and would not forgive you, you know how this situation feels. Have a look at whether your grudge is in reality a way to make someone feel punished. When you withhold love in order to punish, you are inflicting pain and you become the offender.

Maturity and self-growth are required in order to develop compassion for fellow human beings. The journey begins with owning up to the ways you have intentionally or unintentionally hurt others in the past, and it continues by developing compassion for your self. Once you have come this far, you can understand and have compassion for others who have offended as well.

Summoning Your Inner Nurturer

If you still find yourself resenting your apologetic, "yes" category partner, and if are not coming from your parent space of judgment, you may still be regressed into your child pain space. You may be transferring the resentment you feel onto your partner. You must be careful about transferring old issues to the present. A great amount of self-awareness is necessary in order that you not do so. Some wells of pain go deep, indeed, and it may take additional healing work to bleed the charge off of an old pain picture and be in the position to separate the past from the present.

It takes love and compassion for your self to nurture your wounded inner child and to become your own loving parent. It may be difficult to summon your own inner nurturer if you have never been nurtured before. As you weed out the "no" category people from your life, however, and let in the "maybe" and "yes" category people's love and nurturance, you will begin internalizing the energy necessary for your self-soothing. You may need to be surrounded fully by loving and supportive "yes" category energy before you can ameliorate the resentments harbored from the past.

You may also get reacquainted with your own inner child by looking at baby pictures of yourself. When you start the process of feeling your own preciousness and innocence as a baby, the flow of love towards your self is set in motion. You become your own loving parent and give to your self what your inner child is craving.

When your own inner nurturer is accessible, you can summon this wonderful energy when your partner is also in pain. Rather than resist his/her inner child wounds, you will be able to give your partner's inner child loving parental compassion.

Anchoring Yourself in Your Adult Space

The key to reaching a space of forgiveness in relationships is to become anchored in your adult space, which is in present time. From this space, we can achieve understanding because from here we can tune in to the regressed child or to the critical parent spaces others may be coming from when they offend us.

If you understand that all human beings have regressed places, you can have compassion for their hurtful behavior even when it is targeted at you. As long as you do not allow your boundaries to be trespassed when their regressions occur, you can stay in a space of neutrality, see what is happening with clarity, and understand that they are in past-time pain and reacting from a regressed space.

(For an in depth approach and perspective on how to heal deep-seated wounds and reach a space of forgiveness in your life, please refer to Chapter 21, "Epilogue: A Spiritual Philosophy on Forgiveness".)

Chapter 15

COMING FULL CIRCLE: THE SEMI-PERMEABLE BOUNDARY

Have you ever noticed the truly centered person in action? He/she is the person who is always in the observing mode and able to see the jabs and zings thrown at him/her. He/she is the person who does not react defensively, who decides to say something to the offender if the jabs persist relentlessly, but who chooses to let things roll off his/her back when the jabs are from a regressed space on the part of the offender. In doing so, the regressed jabs boomerang back to the offender, while the centered person remains calm and mature.

From his/her space of neutrality, he/she is impervious to zings and slights, and "wins" by coming away from the onslaught "smelling like a rose." He/she successfully keeps out the bad energy by being neutral to it.

On the other hand, he/she is warm and openhearted and able to let in the love that surrounds him/her. He/she projects joy that emanates from within and loves self and life. He/she has a solid sense of self and a semi-permeable, flexible boundary.

Imagine yourself as this person. You are centered, and remain in present time and in your adult space. You have a bubble shield surrounding you. And you have love for your self that emanates from your being.

There exists in your world people you have placed into "no, "maybe" and "yes" categories. You see the energies they emit with clarity, and you stay centered while amidst these energies.

With the "no" categories, you have two options or ways of

responding. The first way is to see the jabs directed at you, and to confront the jabs using the techniques you have learned in order to keep them out of your space. By confronting the energy, you maintain your boundary and you do not let the jabs throw you off center.

The second option is to see the jabs clearly and process your own pain internally, thus letting the jabs bounce off your bubble. You need to see the daggers clearly, or they may penetrate your bubble and throw you off your center and into a regression.

If you stay in the observing mode, your shield can protect you from the zings and daggers, and none of your pictures will be triggered. You will feel healthfully detached from your emotions and yet remain in touch with them because you have shielded yourself from the zings that can make you reel in your emotions.

With the "maybes," you have the same choice of response as with the "no's." However, if a "maybe" person is worth keeping in your inner circle of friends, and if they have "yes" qualities which help them to admit their fault and return to their center, then it is worth sharing your feelings with them when they have jabbed you.

If they respond in the "no" category fashion and become defensive, you have the tools to soothe your self. You have the ability to see their regression clearly and you have compassion for your self. You understand that they are in a regressed space. Your heart may feel slightly closed, because you opened it up to them and they stung you, but when they return to their center and they own their jab with a heartfelt regret, you can open your heart and forgive them.

With the "yes" category people, you can be vulnerable and let in their love. Their intent is to love you, and if your toes are stepped on by these people, they will have compassion for your pain. It is easy to keep your heart open to "yes" people because heartfelt love is the greatest healer of pain.

If you can shield the "no" energy and keep it out of your space by being in the center of your bubble and seeing the energy clearly, if you can soothe yourself when slights occur, and if you can let in love when it comes from the heart, you have successfully built your semi-permeable bubble. You are now in the position to live in peace with your self and others.

Part III
THE METAPHYSICS OF STAYING CENTERED
AND SEEING ENERGY CLEARLY

Chapter 16

TOOLS FOR FEELING SOLID AND CENTERED

The following section describes visualization tools and exercises for helping you feel centered and solid within yourself. Visualization tools will assist you in the process of defending yourself from being thrown off your center by people or situations that you encounter. These visualization tools will also help you to return to your center. They will help you soothe your self when painful memories and unresolved issues are triggered.

The key to staying centered is to become "senior" to energy, rather than allowing energy to control you and throw you off center. The following visualization concepts help to keep you observing both your self, (your inner world), and the outer world, so that you are in charge of the energy in your life, rather than allowing the energy to overwhelm you. The very act of "visualizing energy" keeps you consciously observing both your self and the outer world, so that you do not unconsciously react to situations and people.

The key to "seeing energy clearly" is to be able to trust past experiences and information you have gained without having what may have happened in the past taint the reality of a current situation. Visualization tools help you use information from past experiences while helping you separate your emotions from the experience. In this way, you will be able to see a situation "clearly," and free from distortion.

Finally, visualization tools will help you soothe your self when triggers occur. You will not react to situations from a past-time space when you are able to "see" and locate in your body where the energy affects you, so that you can proactively "remove" the energy from your space.

There are several visualization tools that can assist you in maintaining your centeredness so that you can assess energy accurately. Exercises and tools such as meditation, the "grounding cord and the bubble," and "visualizing what energy looks like," help to keep you centered and in the "observing mode," where you can "see" energy clearly instead of reacting to it. Other tools, such as "blowing up pictures" and "hooking up energy" help to pull you out of your emotion and back to present time when a trigger lights up a picture or memory from your past. "Working with chakras" enables you to locate where in your body you are affected (i.e., which energy centers), allows you to stay separated from the emotions being triggered, and makes it possible for you to gather additional information about the energies that surround and affect you. Finally, using visualization tools for removing "cords" and "daggers," "opening and closing the chakras," and "sending color to your chakras" enables you to proactively soothe and heal your self.

Meditation: Getting in the Body

The essential prerequisite for feeling solid within your self is being present in your body. When you are present and "in your body," you can become aware of the energies surrounding you. You cannot be aware of energy or see energy clearly if you are disconnected from your self and numb to your own feelings. As you move back into your body, you begin to live life in an "awake" and conscious state. Instead of being blinded and numb to energy that surrounds and controls you, you become aware of and sensitive to both the good and the bad energy that can affect you.

Meditation can help you "climb back into your body." If you practice meditation every day, you will be solidifying the "glue" that keeps you solid and centered. Therefore, you will be less susceptible to being knocked off your center by life's waves when they hit.

Setting Up Your Meditation Space

Human beings are creatures of habit. Our bodies respond to routines that we perform habitually. For instance, if you are used to running four miles in the early morning, your body will become used to this. If you miss a day or two, your body will likely feel restless. You are in a routine, and if you break it, your body will go through "withdrawal."

The same principle holds true for meditating. When meditation becomes part of your life, a routine, and if you stop meditating for a day or two, your body will notice the effects. You will not feel as centered. You will be more susceptible to having energy knock you off center. Once you become used to being anchored in your body and living consciously, you will not like the effects of being "out of your body."

Ideally, you will meditate daily. You can start with meditating for fifteen minutes, once in the morning and once in the evening. After a few days to a week, you can increase your interval to a half hour once a day. Over time, you can extend your meditation to an hour or more.

When I have the chance, I give myself a two-hour stretch of deep meditation time. When you remain in trance for that long a period regularly, amazing things begin to happen both internally during the meditation and in your life in general. For example, you may begin to experience a profound inner peace, you may experience communication with a higher spiritual realm, and you may experience metaphysical phenomena. You connect very deeply to your soul and to a level of higher consciousness.

To set up your meditation space, find a comfortable chair and meditate in that chair every day. If you try to meditate while you are lying down, you will probably fall asleep.

Your meditation space needs to be free from the possibility of distraction. Some people like to play music but I personally find this to be distracting. I prefer to listen to the sounds of water such as a waterfall.

Some people like to burn incense or essential oils when they meditate. You need to decide for yourself which aids induce a sense of tranquility in you and what detracts from your tranquility. Ultimately, when you are meditating, you will arrive at a space where everything is tuned out except for the awareness of your being.

Besides making time for a daily meditation (i.e., a half hour in the morning), you may find that during a busy workday, a two-minute break in order to ground your self and to clear your head will be beneficial. You can steal away to the restroom, close the door to your office, sit in your car, or any private place you can find will do in order to close your eyes. If you are feeling scattered or harried during your day, then give yourself a few minutes to return to your center. This can do wonders to keep you centered and feeling present.

The following meditations are provided for you to practice and are based on the metaphysical teachings of Lewis Bostwick (1989). You may wish to tape record them and play the recording back so that you are guided through the meditation. Eventually, you will be able to guide yourself without listening to the tape.

Meditation

Close your eyes and sit comfortably in your chair. Slowly begin to breath in through your nose and out through your mouth. In to the count of three . . . and out to the count of three . . . and in to the count of three . . . and out to the count of three . . .

Say "hello" to your self from the center of your head . . . from behind your eyes. This is your sixth chakra, or "third eye," your place of clairvoyance and the seat of your soul. Say "hello" to your essence . . . the part of you that is eternal . . . breathing in through your nose . . . and out through your mouth . . .

Say "hello" to your grounding cord. Anchor one end of this cord into your first chakra, the energy center at the base of your spine, and anchor the other end of your grounding cord into the center of the planet. You can use a big hook, or anything else you'd like to use, in order to anchor your cord into the planet.

Your grounding cord serves two purposes. One is to serve as a "garbage chute," which allows you to dump any energy that is not yours into your grounding cord and on to the center of the planet, where the energy will neutralize. Your grounding cord also can serve as an anchor, tethering you to the earth's surface. It is like a bungee cord. No matter where you go on the surface of the planet, you will be anchored into the center of the planet by this cord.

Next, imagine a transparent bubble completely enveloping you. It is about three feet above you, beside you, in front of you, behind you, and beneath you. Tuck your bubble into your grounding cord like you would tuck a shirt into a pair of jeans. Your bubble and your grounding cord can penetrate the physical ground because the physical laws that apply to solid matter do not apply to energy.

Now, put a "protection" sign on the outer edge of your bubble that says, "No entrance, please." This sign will protect you from unwanted energy that otherwise would come into your space. It will absorb the energy so that you do not have to use your antennae to scan your environment. Rather, you can sit in the center and let the protection sign ward off the outside energy. You are now completely safe and protected from outside, unwanted energy.

Now visualize a silver tray. Put all the thoughts that are vying for your attention onto this silver platter. Put all the people, projects and things that you are worrying about or thinking about onto this tray. You are going to take a "vacation" from all this for a period of time. You can put your attention back onto these people, projects and things after you come out of this meditation. But for now, place all the things that are going through your mind onto the silver platter, and float this tray away from you, outside of the building. The contents of this tray will be waiting for you after this meditation. You can refocus on them then. But for now, you are taking a vacation from all that and directing your attention only on your self.

Now, imagine a golden sun about three feet above you. This sun is like a magnet that attracts all of your life force energy wherever it may be. Start now to call back all your life force energy. All that is in the past. All that is in the future. Watch your energy being drawn into the sun. It looks like party streamers. As you call back your energy, notice the sun becoming bigger and bigger, as it fills with your life force energy.

Now, open the crown chakra on the top of your head, and let all of the golden energy permeate every single cell of your body and every single space in your bubble. It moves down your face . . . down your neck . . . down your shoulders and your arms. Down your torso . . . and abdomen . . . down your legs and thighs and ankles and feet, and all the way down into your grounding cord.

Bring in one more golden sun of your life force energy and bathe the entire space inside your bubble. Breathe in through your nose . . . and out through your mouth . . . in through your nose . . .and out through your mouth. You are centered, you are calm, you are in a state of peace. Relax in this state and connect with your soul. The part of you that has never died . . . the part that is eternal . . .

(If you are going to be meditating for longer than fifteen minutes, the following part can be added to your meditation).

Running Your Energy

Now say "hello" to your feet chakras . . . the energy vortexes that are on the soles of your feet. Begin now to draw in earth energy from about two miles beneath the surface of the planet, and bring it into the soles of your feet.

Now let the earth energy move up your legs, past your knees . . . past your thighs . . . and into your first chakra at the base of your spine and lower torso. Let the earth energy run down your grounding cord and back into the center of the planet. You are cleaning out your leg channels with grounding, earth energy.

Now open your crown chakra at the top of your head. Begin to draw in "sky" energy that comes from several miles above your head, and let the waterfall of sky energy fall into your crown chakra. Stay in the center of your head and feel the waterfall of energy bathe your face, neck, arms, torso, abdomen, legs, ankles and feet and go all the way down your grounding cord. You are bathing your channels with "sky" energy.

Notice where the "earth" energy and the "sky" energy meet at your first chakra. Your first chakra serves as a pumping station, mixing the two energies. Allow a mixture of ten percent earth energy and ninety percent "sky" energy to flow back up your torso, your neck and your face and out the top of your head, like a whale spout. The mixture can then bathe every space in your bubble and flow down your grounding cord. When the mixture reaches your neck region, allow some of it to flow down your arms. Then the energy will flow out your hands like miniature whale spouts.

You are now "running your energy," and cleaning out your channels with earth and sky vibrations. Do not worry about doing this exercise perfectly. Just keep the energy running through your body. Feel the vibrations moving through your body, how it to relaxes you and cleanses unwanted energy from your space . . .

You will find that running your energy for a longer period of time will induce a deep state of relaxation. You are actually lowering your brain waves from the beta region (waking state) to a deep alpha region, which is the region that your brain waves reach when you are in rapid eye movement (R.E.M.) sleep and are dreaming (Hewitt, 1991). This is a very healing zone. It is a necessary region for your brain to reach. If you are deprived of R.E.M. sleep, you will feel fatigued and disoriented. Conversely, if you practice meditation and increase the amount of time you are in the R.E.M. state, you will notice an improvement in overall well-being, and you will find that you do not need as much sleep. In India, yogis who have trained their brain waves to be in a constant lowered region through meditation have been known to need little or no sleep at all.

Alisa S. Burgess

Your Inner Sanctuary

If you are going to be running your energy for longer than fifteen minutes, the following part, "Going to your inner sanctuary," can be added to your meditation. This part of the meditation allows you to create for yourself and to heal your self. Have fun with this meditation!

Feel the earth and sky energy flow through your body. Say "hello" to your self as you slowly breathe in through your nose and out through your mouth, in through your nose, and out through your mouth . . .

Now open your "sixth chakra," also known as your third eye, which sits behind your eyes in the center of your head. Look out into the huge vastness of the universe. In front of you, you notice a swirling cloud approaching you.

At first, the cloud is red. Allow the red cloud to envelope you. Feel the red vibration move throughout your body as the red cloud swirls around you . . . Now the cloud changes its color to orange. Feel the orange vibration move throughout your body as you allow the orange cloud to swirl around you . . . Notice the cloud now changing to yellow. Feel the yellow vibration flow throughout your body . . . Now the cloud is changing into a peaceful green. Feel the green vibration move throughout your body . . . Ever so gently, the cloud transforms to blue. Feel the blue vibration flowing throughout your body . . . The cloud now transforms to a beautiful, indigo color. Allow the bluish/purple vibration to run through your body . . . The cloud now changes into a soft, violet hue. Feel the violet vibration as you are embraced and surrounded by the soft, violet vibration . . .

Notice that you are starting to swirl around in the whirlpool of the soft, purple cloud. You are beginning to move in a spiral as the cloud lifts you upward . . . higher and higher . . . Very gradually, you notice a shift of direction, and you are now spiraling downward into the funnel of the gentle whirlpool. Feel yourself spiraling down . . . down . . . down . . .

As you reach the bottom of the whirlpool, you land gently on your feet. Notice the purple fog beginning to lift.

You are now in your personal sanctuary. Take a moment to look around this beautiful and magnificent place. Notice the natural waterfall in one part of your sanctuary. Along one stoned wall, there are natural shelves and enclaves with candles burning in them. Notice that the shelves display every imaginable herb and medicine you will ever need to heal your self. Note the sounds and aromas of this beautiful, peaceful haven. Take a look around this magnificent palace. Visualize and create anything you'd like to have here to make this place your sanctuary.

You are perfectly safe here. There is unlimited freedom to create, to play and to heal in this place of wonderment. Take a moment to look around and feel the safety and joy of this place.

Now, move to the center of your sanctuary and sit on the majestic, velvet, down-feathered pillows. Feel yourself sinking in to this soft, comfortable space. Notice a large, home theater movie screen in front of you.

If you wish, using your mind's eye, start to create an image of a goal you would like to accomplish, or a thing you would like to have. Allow this image to appear on your movie screen. Make your goal or wish as specific as possible. If you are visualizing a goal, put the date that you would like this goal to be achieved by beside the image. If you are creating an object to acquire, such as a car or a home, visualize the exact details of this, such as style, color, and so on. Do not limit yourself, for you can ask the Universe for anything you would like. When your creation is exactly as you want it, lift the image off the screen, encase the image in a transparent bubble, and float the bubble out into the universe, where it can accumulate energy to manifest on the physical plane.

You may now wish to give yourself a healing in your inner sanctuary. Look at the wall that houses all the herbs and medicines that you will ever need to be healthy. Allow yourself to use your intuition to pick just the right one to heal yourself. With your mind's eye, ingest this healing medicine and feel yourself feeling healthy and well.

Take a few moments to play in your sanctuary. You can do anything you would like here. If you would like to process feelings, then allow yourself to feel. If you would like to communicate with anyone, then imagine the communication taking place on your movie screen and create the outcome you would like to have. If you would like to send somebody healing or loving energy, then use this space to send positive vibrations to the person on your screen.

There are no limits when you are in your personal sanctuary. Enjoy the freedom of playing by your self, and have fun creating . . .

The Observing Mode:
What Can't Touch You Can't Affect You

While meditation is a tool you can practice in solitude, you will also need some tools to handle energy during normal waking consciousness. The following visualization techniques are offered to help you stay centered while you interact with the world around you.

The "observing mode" is a visualization tool to shield your self from negative energy. You will be shielded from unwanted energy because you are *observing* the energy around you.

As you may recall from chapter eleven, the "observing mode" is your place of neutrality. When you sit in the center of your head and add the component of a bubble shield into your awareness, you can use your bubble to protect your self from outside energy. You will "see" energy bouncing off of your bubble. Therefore, the energy will not touch you or affect you. Instead of *feeling* any triggers, you "*see*" and *observe* the daggers as they bounce off of your bubble.

This place of clarity and neutrality can be referred to as your "sixth chakra," or "third eye." If you are in the observing mode, rather than blindly reacting to the energy, the energy you see can be interpreted objectively.

Say, for instance, that your partner is vehemently reacting to a trigger, and that he/she becomes regressed. As a result, suppose he/she becomes angry and shouts at you. If you are centered behind your bubble, you can literally "watch" the anger bounce off of your shield as you observe him or her in a regressed, child-like space.

To stay in your observing mode, imagine a transparent bubble completely surrounding you. As you may recall, the bubble is above you, in front of you, beside you, behind you, and it tucks into your grounding cord beneath your feet.

Your grounding cord serves to anchor you in present time. The very act of imagining a grounding cord anchored into the center of the real and physical planet serves to remind you that you are awake and conscious and therefore, alert to everything around you.

As you may recall from chapter eleven, when you are grounded and in the center of your bubble, energy literally bounces off of your bubble, and you will be able to clearly see the energy directed towards you. You will be detached from your emotions when you are in your bubble because the bubble deflects the triggers that would normally penetrate your bubble and light up your pictures. What can't touch you can't affect you.

Visualizing the Energy Being Directed Towards You

Another useful tool that enables you to handle energy in an objective manner is to imagine the energy in a tangible form. If someone is angry towards you, for instance, imagine the anger as a color (e.g., red), and let the "red blob" of color splat and bounce off of your bubble. If someone criticizes you, imagine a dagger or knife bouncing off of your shield. If someone who seems sleazy to you is trying to flirt, see the "slime" drip off your bubble.

Have fun with the visualizations. Create your own visions for what different types of energy look and feel like to you. When you visualize the energy in a tangible form, you can separate and detach from the energy and it will not enter your space and trigger you. If you add humor to the visualization, this will be all the better, as humor seems to detach you from your triggers and keep you in a space of neutrality.

Blowing a Picture:
Moving Yourself Back into Present Time

One of the most important visualization tools you can use is that of "blowing a picture" (Bostwick, 1989). This tool is helpful when you are regressed into painful emotions from your past, and when your emotions overwhelm you or cloud your ability to be objective and non-reactive in the present.

"Blowing a picture" enables you to separate your self from your emotions. This technique releases the charge or emotion from your memory and enables you to return to the present time, observing mode, where you can be emotionally neutral to the trigger. If you employ this tool, you will rise above your emotions. As a result, you will not allow them to control and overwhelm you.

Let's suppose that you have been triggered by someone or something and that you feel intense emotion. First, try to locate the picture or memory associated with the feeling. If you cannot, or if you feel you do not have time to find and analyze the picture, you can instead visualize a rose, or any other flower, as a substitute. This image will serve to symbolize the memory.

Second, in order to separate your self from your emotion, in your mind's eye place the image of the memory into a bubble. Now imagine floating the bubble with the image out into the middle of the ocean. Next, in order to take the emotional charge off of the memory, create a bomb beneath the image and "blow it up." The act of blowing up the picture will serve to proactively release the emotion associated with the memory. This will serve to separate your past from the present, enabling you to bring your self back into present time where you are in an emotionally neutral space. You can literally blow a picture in a second or two.

To anchor yourself in present time, imagine a golden sun above your head, and "call back" all of your life force energy from the past and the future into the golden sun. Then open your crown chakra on top of your head and let the golden sun permeate every cell of your body.

An alternative to blowing up a picture or rose is to visualize a Higher Power/Universe/God/Goddess taking the picture and emotion away (Bostwick, 1989). To do this, visualize a large rope (or vine, chain, etc.) with a huge hook on one end. Hook the rope into the bubble that houses the picture, and ask the Higher Power to take it away from your space.

Finally, now that you are in present time, move back into your sixth chakra in the center of your head, where you can observe the situation and respond to it from a neutral, non-reactive position.

For instance, if the person who has triggered you is in the "no" category, you may decide to call this person on his/her behavior from a neutral and non-reactive space. Thus, you can use chapter ten's technique that begins with, "Are you aware that . . ." Or, you may silently observe this person's behavior and see the person clearly, without being knocked off your center. If this person is in the "maybe" or "yes" category, you may wish to share your feelings from a neutral space, using the technique of an "I" message. You might then say, "I felt (adjective) when you said 'such and such'." In either case, you will be responding from a centered and adult space, instead of from an emotionally reactive space.

Overcoming Addictions:
Removing a "Being" from Your Space

The following technique can be used to overcome addictions such as smoking, drinking alcohol and overeating. The technique involves a combination of developing a strong sense of your self through meditation and using the previous tool of "blowing a picture."

In order for the exercise to work, you must truly make the decision to end your addiction. You must meditate on your goal and "program" your goal into your subconscious mind during meditation. No one can make you do anything, including giving up your addiction, unless your core self has made the decision to quit.

Addictions occur when an unconscious part of your self (i.e., your "id," or the part of you that wants immediate gratification), tends to be stronger than your present-time self, or your "ego." You will be able to develop your ego strength as more and more you practice meditation and move back into your body and connect with your core in order to be in present time. Like a snowball that becomes bigger and bigger as it rolls along in the snow, your core will become bigger and stronger as you tune in to and connect with your self through meditation.

To overcome the addiction that has power over you, you will want to imagine the energy that fuels your addiction as being an "entity" that is separate from you. For instance, you might imagine the addictive energy from your "id" as a "smoking being" that looks brown and smoky. Or, imagine the "food being" that causes you to binge as a fat, gelatinous blob.

First, ground and center your self, then put the "being" in a bubble and move the bubble out of your space. Next, put a bomb beneath the bubble and blow it up. Or, you can hook the "being" up to a Higher Power and ask the Higher Power to remove it from your space. Or, you can pour hot oil over the "being," and like the Wicked Witch of the West in *The Wizard of Oz*, you will see the being "melt." Use your imagination to rid the being from your space. In the process, you will be taking charge of your space and overriding your "id" by building your ego strength. You will be operating from your centered space in present time.

When you remove a "being" from your space, you do not want to exert your will. If you try to will the "being" out of your space, you will be going into "resistance." Most likely, the "being" will return, and you will relapse.

Rather, you will want to be in a space of "no effort" and center your self in present time. From a truly centered space, the strong, adult-minded self, who has made the decision to end an addiction, will be in charge, and the energy from your "id," or unconscious, will be effortlessly moved out of your space. The trick is to stay in contact with your core, and move the being out of your space with effortless ease.

The Radar Mode: Using Your Experiences in Your Body

Your body becomes a radar instrument when you use it as a tool for sensing and interpreting incoming energy. The information your body has recorded from earlier experiences is used to assess and interpret incoming information.

For instance, if you are feeling a familiar vibration emanating from someone or something in present time that feels the same as an experience from your past, then use the information, and trust that the vibration indeed is like a vibration you experienced in the past. As an example, if you have been conned by a person in the past and you meet another person in the present who upon your first meeting makes you feel the same way, then trust your radar. Allow your past experience to inform you about this person.

When you use your body as a radar instrument, you must stay with the feelings your body is sensing long enough to be able to connect the feelings with your past experience. You must endure the discomfort of the twinges, flutters and pangs, instead of dissociating or sweeping the feelings under the carpet.

You need to be able to consciously and rationally use your emotions to guide you, however, rather than allow your emotions to overwhelm you and distort your objectivity. If you become immersed in the feelings, you will likely reel with emotion, and this may cause you to overreact to the trigger. If you are not in touch with the experience, the unconscious emotion associated with the repressed memory may cloud and distort your ability to be objective about the present situation. You may then be at risk of blindly transferring your past experience in to the present.

In order to interpret the energy objectively and not transfer your past onto the present, you must become aware of the picture being triggered, separate your self from your emotion, return to your center, and *observe* yourself experiencing the feelings. The visualization technique of "blowing a picture" can be used to pull your self out of an emotion and back into present time. If you know how to blow a picture, you will then be equipped to use your past experiences as your guide without having the emotions from the past cloud your vision or overwhelm you in the present.

Some people fear that if they move back into their bodies and get more in touch with their emotions and past memories, they will be stuck in their pain and never return to a centered place. It is scary for them to become connected to their emotions and memories because their emotions have overwhelmed and controlled them for so long.

But it is tragic to be split off from all the information your soul has gained throughout life. If in your past, for instance, you have been molested and have dissociated from the experience, or you have repressed the experience into your unconscious, you will not be able to use this information in order to recognize a molester if you encounter one today. When we embrace our past experiences and emotions, we have a wealth of information available to us. Experience in fact can be our greatest guide.

To use your body as a radar instrument, you must trust what your body is telling you. In order for you to feel a twinge, flutter or pang, or in order for a past-time picture to be triggered, something outside you that is real must be responsible. All your discomfort is not coming from inside.

To use your body as a radar instrument, you must first feel the emotion that is triggered. For example, suppose you have been molested as a child and you are interviewing a pedophile for a nanny position in present time. Allow your self to feel your discomfort and fear in the presence of this person.

Second, locate the picture/memory associated with the feeling. In this case, you would link the fear and discomfort that you feel in the present with the memory of you being molested. This picture will give you information about the person/trigger in the present situation, as the feelings will be of the same vibration. In order to move your self out of the picture and emotion from your past, you would then "blow the picture" and pull your attention back into present time.

Finally, trust the information gleaned from your past experience. You can then deal with the present-time person/trigger from a neutral position. For instance, you may wish to confront the energy using the technique of an "I" message to state your truth and say, "I feel uncomfortable with you babysitting my children." Or, you can use the powerful tool of seeing the person clearly behind your bubble/shield, silently observing him/her in action, and take the appropriate precautions, such as not offering the person the position.

When you use your body as a radar instrument in conjunction with returning to your sixth chakra and being inside your bubble in present time, you will be able to use the accumulated information of your past to see energy clearly. You will not be blindly transferring past experience to the present. Nor will you be thrown off your center. You can then effectively handle the energy from a neutral and present-time space.

A word of caution is in order. When you use your body as a radar instrument, if you are "stuck" in a past-time picture, you will be unable to separate your self from the emotion, and your ability to assess a situation objectively and accurately will be impaired. Anytime you feel a vehement charge or intensity of emotion from a trigger and you cannot pull yourself out of the emotion and return to a neutral space, you are stuck in a past-time picture. If you have a strong emotion that does not subside, it is a likely and valid clue that you are stuck in a past-time picture that you have not yet resolved. The information from this picture will then distort the reality of the current situation.

You will then need to soothe you own inner child or heal the picture through processing or therapy in order to take the charge off of the picture. Remember, only a small portion of the emotional charge from the trigger is coming from the present. The majority of the emotional charge is usually coming from a past-time picture.

Chapter 17
CHAKRAS:
ENERGY VORTEXES THAT HOUSE YOUR INFORMATION

The "chakra system" is an extremely useful conceptual tool that involves the idea of chakras, or energy centers that make up your being. When you become familiar with how to use of the chakra system, you will know when boundary violations occur and will be able to identify the specific energies that affect you.

Initially, when you become familiar with the chakra system, you will be able to visualize and interpret outside energy and the affect the energy may have over you, while staying in your observing mode. Due to the fact that you are visualizing outside energy affecting your various energy centers, you will be able to observe your self experiencing your feelings, rather than plummet into your emotions.

As you move into your body and become more sensitive to energy, however, you will actually be able to physically *feel* your chakras being affected. You will then be able to use the chakra system to identify what you are feeling, and from whom or where the energy is coming.

The chakras are energy vortexes that metabolize incoming energy for you to process and make sense of. There are seven major chakras in your body. Each one is associated with a specific category of information.

The first chakra is associated with information pertaining to survival and security issues, such as food clothing and shelter. The second chakra is associated primarily with sexual matters. The

161

third chakra is associated with issues involving will and power. The fourth houses information pertaining to having compassion for one's self and others and about matters of the heart. The fifth chakra relates to communication issues and the ability to speak your truth. The sixth relates to the ability to see things clearly and to separate the truth from the lie. Finally, the seventh chakra relates to issues involving certainty and "knowing things off the top of your head" (Bostwick, 1989).

There is a growing body of literature that suggests that the human body stores memory of experiences in the body tissue (Brennan, 1989). Let us postulate that experiences you have had throughout your life have been recorded somewhere in your body.

Each experience has a memory and emotion attached to it. Together, the memory and the emotion form a "picture."

Each picture is housed in the specific chakra that pertains to the category of information associated with the chakra's function. For example, if you have a picture that involves sexual abuse, it will be stored in your second chakra, which is the center for housing sexual information.

If you are familiar with the categories of information that correspond to each chakra, and if someone triggers you, then it will be possible to locate the specific chakra that is affected. You will be able to "see" the energy and be able to soothe your self by visualizing your self removing the offending energy from your chakra. The very act of visualizing the energy helps you to stay detached from your emotions. The act of visualizing puts you in the position of an observer witnessing your self experiencing your emotions, and this keeps you from plummeting into them.

If you know the type of information that is associated with each particular chakra, for instance your voice being squelched (5th chakra - throat), or someone flirting with you (2nd chakra – pelvic region), you then will be able to work with the chakra to "see" and remove the energy. As you become more sensitive to energy and move more into your body, you may actually feel the physical area of the chakra being affected.

For instance, let's say that someone or something triggers the feeling in you that you cannot speak up or state your truth. Let's suppose that you are familiar with the chakra system and know that the fifth chakra is located in the throat and is the center of communication and speaking your truth. You are now equipped to visualize some sort of energy that is blocking this chakra and affecting your ability to speak. Or, you may actually feel a "frog in your throat," or your throat tightening. You are now able to visualize yourself removing the cords or daggers that have been thrown into your fifth chakra. The act of visualizing yourself removing the cords puts you back in control, so that now you can proactively do something about speaking up.

You may then take a look at the "pictures" housed in the throat region and find a past memory that blocked your ability to speak up. For instance, you may remember being punished or humiliated as a child for saying what you felt. Finding the picture helps you maintain an inner dialogue between you and your triggers. By staying in the observing mode, you are able to achieve a degree of emotional distance from the triggers. If you can "blow" this picture and return to present time, you will have successfully taken control away from your past experience. You will also be better able to see the source of the trigger and how whatever it was is attempting to control you.

To visualize the chakra system, imagine that you are a perpendicular pole. Imagine seven energy vortexes situated from the base of your spine to the top of your head. Imagine that each vortex has a special function and quality of energy that it metabolizes and pumps through your energy field.

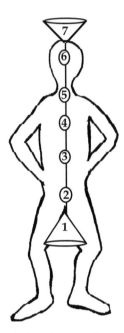

The Chakra System: Front View

The first and seventh chakra can be conceptualized as whirlpools of energy that look like a funnel or tornado. The narrow part of the first chakra's whirlpool is connected to the chakra at the base of the spine and the wide part of the funnel extends downward towards the earth. The narrow part of the seventh chakra's whirlpool is connected at the crown of your head and the wide part of the funnel extends upward towards the heavens (Brennan, 1987).

The second, third, fourth, fifth and sixth chakras can be conceptualized as a pair of whirlpools of energy that look like funnels or tornadoes. Each whirlpool opens and closes like a vegetable steamer. One whirlpool of each chakra is on your front, and the other whirlpool is on the backside of you. The narrow ends of the pair of whirlpools connect into the backbone and the wide ends of the pair of whirlpools extend outward in front or behind you (Brennan, 1987).

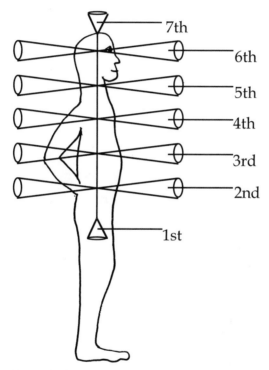

7th

6th

5th

4th

3rd

2nd

1st

The Chakra System: Side View

One whirlpool draws in energy from the world in front of you and into the base of its chakra at its respective place along the backbone while the other whirlpool draws in energy from behind you and into the base of the chakra at its corresponding point along the backbone (Brennan, 1987). Hence, each chakra, with its pair of whirlpools, draws in specific information that corresponds to its chakra from the world and pumps it through your energy field by way of the channel running up your backbone. For more information of the chakra system, I recommend Barbara Ann Brennan's thorough book, *Hands of Light: A Guide to Healing Through the Human Energy Field* (1987).

The First Chakra

The first chakra sits at the base of your spine. Its primary function is to deal with energy associated with your basic survival. Issues and concerns about food, clothing, shelter, finances and keeping the body alive are subjects of the first chakra. If you are starving, if you lose your job, if your home is destroyed in a fire or earthquake, or if you are ill, your first chakra will be "lit up" and will become wide open. Likewise, if you are walking down the street and a bus swerves and almost hits you, your first chakra will automatically open wide as your body goes into "fight or flight" survival mode, bringing in energy to light up information housed in your first chakra in order to keep your body alive.

Ordinarily, your first chakra should be about ten percent open, or just enough to keep the body in healthy balance. If you open you first chakra too much, adrenaline will pump through your body, stimulating the "fight or flight" response. When you are anxious, it will help to consciously close down your first chakra to the ten percent position by using your imagination.

Often, people may attempt to control you through your first chakra. If your partner has a penchant for threatening to leave you, you may sense a tug in the region of your first chakra, and you may feel the ensuing panic or anxiety when this chakra opens wide.

Likewise, if your boss threatens to lay you off, the first chakra will open wide and you will feel the resulting anxiety. If you are informed of a diagnosis of cancer, your first chakra will also "light up" and open.

The antidote for ameliorating first chakra anxiety is to soothe your self by visualizing yourself closing the chakra back down to the ten percent position. In addition, you need to find the survival pictures or memories that are housed in your first chakra information center. When you locate these pictures, you can release emotion from the memory by "blowing a picture." If it is helpful to you, you can use the information from the memory and pull yourself back into "present time."

Many people have written about the relationship between the chakras and our physical bodies and illness. In *You Can Heal Your Life* (1984), Louise Hay discusses how our thoughts create our illnesses, and proposes that our illnesses are bodily metaphors for what we repudiate, fear and resist. She suggests specific affirmations to repeat to your self in order to heal the illness created by the erroneous thoughts and messages we send ourselves.

The region in your body which houses the first chakra would then be associated with issues that are first chakra concerns. For instance, survival and security issues might manifest themselves as lower back problems. According to Louise Hay, if you have a lower back problem, you may have a "fear of money" or "lack of financial support," in which case she would suggest you to repeat to yourself the affirmation, "I trust the process of life. All I need is always taken care of. I am safe" (Hay, 1984).

In her ground breaking book, *Hands of Light: Healing Through the Human Energy Field* (1987), Brennan bridges scientific research with metaphysical literature, and discusses the correlation between frequency/wave patterns, colors, and chakras. She cites one study on the human aura, "Project Report: A Study of Structural Integration from Neuromuscular, Energy Field, and Emotional Approaches," that was conducted by Dr. Valerie Hunt, W. Massey, R. Weinberg, R. Bruyere, and P. Hahn at UCLA in 1977.

In this study, electrodes were used to record low millivoltage signals from the body during a series of rolfing, or deep tissue massage sessions. The wave patterns were scientifically recorded by a Fourier analysis and sonogram frequency analysis. During these rolfing sessions, Reverend Rosalyn Bruyere, a clairvoyant aura reader from the Healing Light Center in Glendale, California, used her psychic vision, and simultaneously recorded her impressions of the color, size and movements of the chakras and auric clouds. The wave patterns were then mathematically analyzed by scientists.

Amazingly, the colors and specific location named in the aura by Reverend Bruyere consistently correlated with the scientifically recorded frequency/wave patterns for those colors. The same results were obtained when Dr. Hunt repeated the experiment with seven other aura readers. As an example, the scientific measurements would always show the characteristic blue wave pattern and frequency in the same locations that the auric readers had observed the blue to be located (Brennan, 1987).

Moreover, Dr. Hunt noted that the colors associated with the chakras in the metaphysical literature frequently corresponded with the colors recorded in the body's chakra regions. For example, she noted red for the kundalini, orange for hypogastric, yellow for the spleen, green for the heart, blue for the throat, violet for the third eye, and white for the crown (Brennan, 1987).

Hence, in line with the metaphysical literature, the color red is

associated with the first chakra (Brennan, 1987). If you are
of some grounding in your life, you may consider wearing t
red to bring in the vibration associated with first
information. Or you may try visualizing bringing the color
your first chakra in order to replenish and balance this energy

The Second Chakra

The second chakra sits in the abdomen about two inche
the navel. The second chakra is concerned with issues concer
as well as the emotions. All your sexual information is hous
Anything that has to do with your sexual relationships, or
others by empathizing and feeling their pain as if it were yo
is a product of this chakra (Bostwick, 1989).

Your second chakra will be lit up, for example, if yo
information about how to deal with the sexual aspe
relationship. It will be closed down if you are avoiding
aspects of your life. Any information about sexual bo
violations, such as molestation, incest or rape will be stored
region of your body.

Likewise, if you are an "empath" and feel others' emotio
they were your own, then you are using your second chakra
others. You will be bringing others' pain into your own sp
order to heal their pain. Remember, however, it is *not* desir
have other people's energy inside of your own space, as f
energy blocks the ease and flow of your own energy, causing
ease."

More desirable spaces from which to heal others are th
your heart chakra, or space of compassion, or through your
chakra, or space of clarity and understanding. These are a
healthy alternative for you. Both of these spaces keep you sep

rom the person you are healing and your boundary and energy low intact.

When you are in a sexual relationship with another, a cord of energy connects the two of you at your second chakras (Bostwick, 1989). It comes as no surprise that if a lover cheats on you, and if you are in your body and connected to your soul, you will feel the betrayal when it is happening. I have had many cases of patients over the years who have woken in the middle of the night because they feel a tug, panic or disconnect. They sensed their partner kissing or making love to another and later discovered that their intuition and fear were correct (e.g., they found physical evidence or the partner confessed).

In other situations, however, a person's second chakra fears of infidelity may be "lit up" as they are opening their second chakras to a trustworthy "yes" person. The fears must come from somewhere, so something in present time must be triggering the picture. Thus, the person must take a look at their past-time pain, harbored as "pictures" in their second chakra. The pictures may come from an experience where one parent betrayed the other, or they may come from a bad prior relationship. The couple must take a look at what one partner is doing that triggers the fear pictures in the other.

If the partner is not doing anything to trigger the picture (e.g., flirting with another), then it may be an instance where a "corrective emotional experience" is happening. If this is the case, then the old "daggers" are reverberating and causing fear because the person is opening up the chakra even though it is to let in the "yes" category, good energy. In the process of opening the heart in a safe relationship, old, embedded daggers are exposed and "lit up." In this way they can be felt and healed.

As you become aware of the pictures housed in your second chakra, you can use this past information to navigate your way through present-time relationships. The following case illustrates how one woman, through a present-time relationship, became familiar with her feelings surrounding a past molestation.

An uncle molested this woman when she was very young. While my patient was aware of the incident, she was innocent, naive and trusting towards that particular type of perpetrator energy, as though she were still that little child of long ago.

The trauma picture served as a "magnet" to attract a similar vibration to her in order for the past-time picture to be "lit up" and healed. She attracted a man into her life who had been a long-time, platonic friend. One night, during a summer solstice celebration, he forced himself on her and she became a victim of date rape. After the incident, however, she continued to be friends with him.

The lessons she needed to learn through this experience were two-fold. She needed to learn to listen to her gut feelings about this man's integrity and to set boundaries for her self. She also needed to learn how not to abandon her self by overriding her angry and disappointed feelings. He had no regard for her boundaries and she gave him too much slack.

Over time, she set better boundaries for herself, and began to vocalize how she felt about the date rape to her male friend. As she vocalized her feelings, she was able to feel more profoundly the disappointment and anger towards her uncle for violating her innocence and trust. She was also able to feel the pain of having abandoned her soul to these predators in order to maintain a connection with them. Ultimately, she learned what predator energy felt like in conscious and present-time space, so that she could feel what her gut what telling her and be in position to refuse that type of relationship should it happen to enter her life again.

The next case is another example that illustrates an issue to do with the second chakra. A woman had repressed a molestation memory and the picture attracted a similar vibration in order to "light up," heal and neutralize her molestation picture.

A women's father was abusive and a con man. The woman did not believe she had been the target of his physical abuse, but she had been a witness to his violent temper, which he took out on her brothers, sister and live-in cousin.

When she was in college, she felt an immediate attraction to a man and they dated for a brief period of time. This man later turned out to be a criminal rapist. She discovered this while reading the local newspaper. Later, she began to have dreams that her father had molested her. The picture in her space had attracted a similar vibration in the form of the rapist in order for her to consciously re-experience what had happened to her when she was a child.

Our unconscious pictures may also attract a situation that a parent had to deal with so that we can find the truth about a situation. For example, a woman's father cheated on her mother with her mother's best friend. Even though the father married his lover shortly after the divorce, the father adamantly denied that he had been having an affair. As a result, the woman became confused, and she lost certainty about her ability to see the truth. She didn't know whether to believe herself or her father.

The woman's truth resided in her second chakra. Her pictures there attracted relationships into her life in which she was deceived and betrayed by her partners, just as her mother had been. She was finally able to become consciously aware of the truth after she began to trust her feelings and her intuition concerning a partner's philandering character. She was no longer blinded by lies. She was then able to set boundaries for herself and to confront the partner's behavior, which her mother had not been able to do.

Years later, her father finally alluded to his affair. Unconsciously, she had known the truth about her father's infidelities all along. She'd had to go through some painful relationships of her own, however, in order to consciously experience what betrayal felt like. This enabled her to find her truth and to trust her truth.

When someone "cords" you in the second chakra, his or her energy is causing a picture in your second chakra to reverberate, as in the previous cases of a predator lighting up molestation pictures. Or, the person is revving up your chakra and trying to get your attention by flirting with you. If you recognize when your second chakra is corded, you will be able to stay centered and respond to the energy in the way that you wish to respond, that is, from a conscious, aware space. If, however, you are not aware when your second chakra is corded, you will be prone to being knocked off your center and to reacting from an unaware space.

Illnesses in the second chakra region of the body may relate to second chakra concerns. For example, if you have testicular, uterine, or ovarian pain, you may want to tune in to issues concerning sexuality or relationships. For example, according to Louise Hay, female problems such as dysmenorrhea and fibroid tumors relate to "denial of the self" and/or "rejecting femininity." Vaginitis relates to "anger at a mate," "sexual guilt" or "punishing the self," and testicles relate to "masculine principles" and "masculinity" (Hay, 1984). What metaphor is your body communicating to you through your second chakra pain?

The color orange is associated with the second chakra (Brennan, 1988; Cohen, 1988). If you find your sexual appetite to be in overdrive and detrimental to your life, you may discover that closing your second chakra down a bit, or visualizing a cooler color to tone down the heat of the orange, to be helpful. If you have a lowered libido, you may find that wearing orange or bringing orange into your second chakra aids in opening the chakra. If you find yourself healing others' pain by empathizing and feeling the pain as if it were your own, then closing down your second chakra and moving your focus into your fourth and sixth chakra centers is advised.

The Third Chakra

The third chakra is located in your solar plexus, about three inches above your navel. Energies concerning will, personal power, control and competition are the domain of the third chakra. Someone who wishes to manipulate you will attempt to do so by cording your third chakra. If a boss is undermining you, your third chakra will be lit up. If someone is in competition with you, they will try to "whack" you in the third chakra and "knock the wind out of your sails."

One of my patients was involved in individuating from his family. The family lived in the South and he lived in California. He had a Master's degree from a reputable private college and was a nutrition and yoga teacher at a local college. One reason that he had moved to California was that he had an interest in spirituality and metaphysics. He had heard that California has many like-minded people. He longed for a deep connection from his family members and wanted them to accept and honor his values. He felt wonderful when they would say, "We love you and miss you."

A family event offered an opportunity for him to fly to see the family for a weekend. However, on the morning of the flight, his third chakra felt as though it were wide open. He wondered if he should listen to his body. It was a difficult decision to make but in the end he canceled his flight and honored what his body was telling him. His third chakra was saying that if he went, he would feel completely controlled by his family. He would feel invalidated and judged because of his philosophical and spiritual viewpoints. The only way his family would approve of him would be for him to abandon his identity in order to fit into their conservative and limited view of what was acceptable. Whenever he would share good news about the progress of a project he was working on, they would invalidate him by saying that he was "unscholarly." When an individual is forced to abandon self and is controlled by others, the third chakra (and perhaps your stomach, intestines, etc.) will feel the effects.

The color associated with the third chakra is yellow (Brennan, 1987; Cohen, 1988). If ever you feel lethargic and lacking in will and personal power, visualize the color yellow permeating your third chakra. This may bring the energetic charge you need. If you find yourself being bossy and dominating, you may need to cool down the third chakra a bit by imagining a cooler vibration, such as blue.

Gordon Gekko, the character played by Michael Douglas in the movie, "Wall Street," primarily operated through his third chakra. He was interested in power and had no regard for the welfare of others. He was interested in knocking down the competition and staying on top. He also operated through his second chakra, and was interested in women for sex but not for meaningful relationships. Finally, he operated through his first chakra, in that he was driven by greed.

The lower three chakras are sometimes negatively referred to as the "Money, Sex, and Power" houses of the vices of man. When people live only in the lower three chakras, they may indeed be under the control of the negative vibrations of a limited world. In order to raise your vibrations and expand your universe, you must balance the energies in the lower three chakras so that you are not stuck in the survival mode, controlled by greed, relating to others exclusively as sexual objects, and/or competing with others and knocking out their boundaries. If you enjoy balance in your own life and have reverence for others' boundaries, then you will be able to raise your vibrations and remain comfortably in the higher vibrations of the fourth, fifth, sixth, and seventh chakras.

The Fourth Chakra

The fourth chakra is located in the heart area in the center of your chest. The fourth chakra is sometimes referred to as the "heart" chakra, and it is the "home of compassion" and "love" for both your self and others.

The first key to achieving a life of joy and fulfillment is to love your self. When you truly love, embrace and accept all aspects of your self, then you can truly have compassion for others. If there is something you do not accept about your self, then you will judge and be critical of others who have the same trait. Whenever you judge others, you are judging your self at some level.

Your heart is slightly closed when you judge your self or others. It does not feel good to have the heart closed, as the heart is the center for giving and receiving love, and the body thrives on love.

The ultimate stance to attain is to have your heart open to all, and at the same time to protect your self from "no" category energy with your bubble/shield. If you do not have a bubble, however, or if it is developing but not yet gelled, then closing down the heart chakra is a way to keep out "no" category energy.

"No" category energy often whacks its victim's fourth chakra. The "best" way for someone to control you and knock you off your center is to "split your affinity for your self" and cause you to feel badly about yourself. If you don't like something about your self, then that something becomes an Achilles heel for the "no" category energy to judge, punish, criticize, reject, or ridicule. You will then be thrown off your center and you will reel in self-doubt and low self-esteem.

On the other hand, if you have embraced and accepted all aspects of your self, including your looks, your weight, your intelligence, your quirks, your personality etc., then you will be impervious to the zings the "no" category energy throws at you. If you accept your foibles with loving kindness and humility, then others won't be able to punish your foibles, for you have given your self the love you need. This love serves as a protection from negative energy.

You may have heard of the children's rhyme, "Sticks and stones may break my bones, but names will never hurt me." This may be true for a person with high self-esteem. Nevertheless, perhaps the most detrimental thing you can do to a person is to intentionally and sadistically hurt her/him through "name calling" (i.e., ridiculing, teasing, criticizing, judging, etc.) The body can heal itself, but the emotional scars that are left from whacking someone's fourth chakra can be severe. It may take a very long time to heal the dagger wounds inflicted upon an unprotected soul, and the victim will suffer from low self-esteem and a broken or wounded heart.

The following case illustrates the sorrowful effects that sadistic energy can have on one's fourth chakra. This woman was born in Russia and moved to America when she was eight. She began her career as an author writing children's books and later became a pediatric nurse. Her best friend and sorority sister in college lived near her. For twenty-five years, their families had gotten together socially.

The best friend divorced her husband. Then she betrayed her sorority sister, the pediatric nurse, by having an affair with the nurse's husband. During this secret affair, the best friend shopped for a birthday gift for the nurse that would be given to her by her husband. The nurse was thirty pounds overweight, and the "best friend" bought a bathrobe for her in a "petite small" size. Moreover, the "best friend" and husband made her try the robe on in front of them and laughed at her when the robe did not fit. The "best friend" went on to marry the nurse's husband.

The nurse's fourth chakra was whacked several times by her husband and the "best friend." The nurse had always been sensitive about her weight, making the sadistic energy attached to the petite sized robe extremely hurtful to her self-esteem and to her spirit. Moreover, the act of the husband and "best friend" making her try the robe on in front of them was especially humiliating. As you might imagine, the fact that the "best friend" betrayed her made her furious. The fact that the husband betrayed her made her feel worthless and unloved.

The nurse never quite healed from the pain of the betrayal. Interestingly, her father had had an affair with his business partner's wife, and later married the woman. The pain picture of her father's infidelity attracted the same situation into her life for her to resurrect and feel. While the affair/infidelity picture may have been housed in her second chakra area of her body (indeed she had fibroids in her uterus which may have been related to this emotional pain), the pain of her broken heart was most devastating. She died of a heart attack many years later. I am forced to wonder to what extent her broken heart caused by her husband and her "friend" contributed to her heart attack.

The fourth chakra is the center of compassion and love. It is through our hearts that we give and receive love. Love and compassion are the foundation of "yes" category energy. The energies of love and compassion are unequivocally healing and nourishing. Letting love into your heart can heal the soul's wounds.

When you give the energy of love from your heart, however, you must keep your energy field replenished. You must be aware of your bubble/boundary and not take another person's pain into your space to heal, (i.e., by using your second chakra and empathizing with their pain and feeling it as if it is your own). If you do take on their pain, you risk depleting your field and becoming ill. Moreover, it is not your job to take someone else's pain away from them in order to heal it, or to solve their problems for them. When you do, you are interfering with their life path and the lessons that they need to learn.

You can, however, *sympathize* with their pain and express genuine concern and love for them while they are feeling their pain. You must allow yourself to tolerate them feeling their pain. Do not take their feelings away from them or you will be denying them the chance to enter a pain picture and move more firmly into their body.

The color associated with the fourth chakra is green (Brennan, 1988; Cohen, 1988). Green is a wonderful healing color. Use it to replenish your heart. If you find yourself judging someone (as opposed to making an assessment of them from a neutral space), then visualize filling your heart with green, and visualize sending him or her a bubble of green energy. This technique has some amazing results in turning energy around to a more loving space.

The Fifth Chakra

The fifth chakra is located in the region of your vocal cords in the center of your throat. Its primary function is to deal with energies associated with communication and speaking your truth. If you are silenced, your fifth chakra has been "whacked." If you "walk on eggshells" around a potentially volatile person, then she/he is controlling you and silencing you by blocking your fifth chakra. If you find yourself tongue-tied or stuttering around a particular person or energy, then that energy is controlling your fifth chakra.

In each of the above scenarios, *you* have the power to energetically remove their cords of control and to own your fifth chakra again. As you are working on individuation issues and removing the fear of others' anger, punishment, abandonment, rejection, ridicule etc., you will remove the chains that bind your vocal cords, and will be able to speak your truth.

If you speak your truth from the centered space using "I" messages, then whatever energy ensues will be valuable information for categorizing the person into the "no," "maybe," or "yes" categories. If the person leaves, if the person fires you, or if some other seemingly negative consequence occurs as a result of you speaking your truth, then the Universe is correcting a situation for you, so that you will not have to remain shackled and enslaved. Another person or job will come along that is even better if you will take a risk and speak your truth so that the new and better vibration that does not shackle you can enter your life.

The best environment is one in which you can speak your truth and have that truth respected, heard, honored or understood. Remember, however, that you should not always expect your truth to be agreed with. Each of us has his/her own truth.

"What about office politics?" you may ask. Often you find yourself in a dysfunctional work environment where you see the energy clearly, yet you would "cut off your nose to spite your face" if you really spoke up and said your truth. In this situation, you are your best guide in determining whether it is wise or prudent to speak your truth. You must also be honest with your self and assess whether this is the best work environment for you. If you compromise your self and say to your self that you see the situation clearly, and you consciously chose to be the observer while you collect your pay check, then that may be fine for a while. But watch out for fifth chakra blockages that may relate to physical illness, such as thyroid problems, laryngitis, tonsillitis or a sore throat. In the end, you must ask yourself, "On my path towards spiritual freedom, is this the most conducive environment for me?"

I had a Japanese patient in her late fifties who was struggling with the issue of speaking her truth to authority figures. While this woman was extremely intelligent and had a Master's degree in childhood development, she had little self-confidence, and worked as an overnight attendant in a home for emotionally challenged adults.

She had two distinct voices that she would use as she spoke to me. One voice was a very beautiful and mature voice that had a soothing resonance and lower register tone. Her other voice was high pitched, and like that of a little girl's.

She was intimidated by her boss and had difficulty speaking her mind. Through the course of our work together, she was able to move through the fear of speaking her truth, and "blew up" some childhood fear pictures as she confronted both her mother and her boss. She decided to move on from that job and is now living and working in a new environment that is much more conducive to her truth. She rarely uses her child voice anymore, and if she does, she is aware that her voice is being squelched by some energy. She can therefore, move the oppressing energy out of her space and speak her truth.

I attended a spiritual retreat several years ago to learn about Ojibwe tribal healings. The American Indian tribe has a beautiful ceremony of passing the "truth stick" around the circle, and as each member speaks and shares, he/she is holding the truth stick. When you are holding the truth stick, your fifth chakra becomes open and your true feelings and soul emerge for all to connect with. It is a most healing experience to be heard in an atmosphere of complete acceptance and non-judgment. If you will surround yourself with "yes" category people and open your fifth chakra, any risk you may take in doing so will well be worth the heavenly experience you will receive.

The color associated with the fifth chakra is blue (Brennan, 1988; Cohen, 1988). Use this color to clear out your fifth chakra when control energy of any type silences your vocal cords.

The Sixth Chakra

The sixth chakra is located in the center of your head, behind your eyes. Imagine a line going from one ear through your head to the other ear. Next, find the spot behind your eyes that intersects the ear-to-ear line. That point in the center of your head is the sixth chakra.

The sixth chakra is your place of clairvoyancy, which literally means "clear vision." The sixth chakra is also referred to as the "third eye." The primary function of the sixth chakra is to see clearly, and to separate the truth from a lie. If you are tricked, deceived or conned, then someone has blinded your sixth chakra.

One movie that I cite in my work with people is "Gaslight." In this movie, the husband attempts to make his wife believe she is going insane. The husband makes his wife doubt her perceptions by crawling in the attic rafters during the night and turning the gas in the gas lamps off and on. Then he returns to the room where his wife is sitting, and denies noticing any strange occurrences. When someone intentionally tries to distort your reality and to blind you to the truth in order to control you, I call this type of attempted control of the sixth chakra "gas lighting."

I believe that illnesses are messages and metaphors that our bodies use to try to communicate something to us. Either the message is attempting to nudge us back onto our spiritual path, or the illness is there for the experiences it causes others to feel who are in our wake. I believe that every experience has a lesson attached to it, and while it may not be entirely accurate to say that we create our illnesses, it is helpful to realize that whatever the cause of our illness may be, we can learn something from it.

My own experience began with the diagnosis of a pituitary micro adenoma, or a small tumor, that sat in front of my sixth chakra in the center of my head. The pituitary is the master gland that regulates hormones. It sits on the optic chiasm where the optical nerves cross over and connect to the brain.

The tumor was diagnosed by an MRI scan, and medication was prescribed to keep the tumor from secreting a hormone called prolactin. I took the medication for about a week and did not like how it made me feel (e.g., clouded and with a headache).

I then attended a lecture by a wise and spiritual clairvoyant named Lewis Bostwick. Lewis was the founder of the Berkeley Psychic Institute. He gave this lecture one evening in San Francisco.

At this lecture, I asked about the nature of my tumor. I said I wanted to know if he could offer any information based on anything that he could "see." He said that the tumor, which was in the sixth chakra, was created by energy that was meant to blind me from the truth about what was going on in my family when I was growing up. One parent was having an affair and one parent was afraid of losing custody over me, so neither parent wanted me to see the truth about the situation, and as a result, I was "blinded."

At that point, I felt an affinity with my micro adenoma, as ridiculous as that sounds. I realized that my path was to move the energy that was blinding my clarity out of my space. I began to enter back into my body and began to feel the pain of my past. I had been disconnected from my feelings and "in my head" from studying in undergraduate and graduate school, and I never really allowed myself to feel the pain of the past. As I began to confront the family secrets and lies, and as I endured the fallout that ensued during my journey of individuation, my symptoms improved and my ability to see reality expanded.

The micro adenoma, and the journey it took me on, taught me the truth about certain energies that were in my life. If it had not occurred I might not be writing this book today. As a result of it, I was introduced to a spiritual philosophy that I was able to combine with my clinical knowledge. The culmination of this is this knowledge that I am sharing with you today.

The color associated with the sixth chakra is indigo blue (Brennan, 1987; Cohen, 1988). If you find yourself in a fog and lacking perspective, you may find it helpful to visualize yourself clearing your third eye with the indigo color. If you doubt your self and lose your certainty, it is likely that someone else is distorting your truth and clouding your perceptions. Take a look at the cord of energy that is stuck in your sixth chakra, and see who has blinded you. Then visualize yourself removing the cord, and visualize yourself giving it back to its owner. Then bring in the golden sun of your own life force energy and replenish your space with this energy.

The Seventh Chakra

The seventh chakra is located on top of your head. For this reason, the seventh chakra is also referred to as the "crown" chakra. Imagine a funnel with the narrow end in your head and the wide part up towards the sky. The seventh chakra draws energy into your body from above.

The seventh chakra is concerned with higher truth, having "seniority over your own space," and knowing things "off the top of your head" (Bostwick, 1989). When you are using your seventh chakra, you do not have to analyze things. Rather, you just "know." It has been said that the noun "knowingness" was created to designate information obtained through the seventh chakra (Bostwick, 1989).

If you ever find yourself being controlled by an energy with an aura of authority and you feel subservient, less knowing, or controlled, take a look at who is cording your seventh chakra. Identify the source, find the picture/memory associated with the feeling of being corded by this energy, "blow" the pictures, remove the cord and return it to its owner. When you use this type of visualization, you succeed in regaining the power of your own space. The very act of playing around with this type of visual game keeps you aware and alert to the energies around you so that the energies are not controlling you.

The color associated with the seventh chakra is violet (Brennan, 1987; Cohen, 1988) to white (Brennan, 1987) to gold (Bostwick,

1989). Use this color to clear out your crown chakra and to take charge of your own space.

Chapter 18

USING THE CHAKRA SYSTEM:
SOOTHING YOUR SELF

Now you are familiar with the seven major chakras and the categories of information they store in your body. When you know the chakra system, you can use the category grid to identify where in your body you are feeling a particular type of energy (e.g., third chakra region when you are being manipulated or controlled). You will then be able to stay in the observing mode and visualize the energy that is affecting you, and you will be consciously aware of the energy that triggers you.

Let's review the chakra grid again. Situations, people, and other triggers that relate to basic survival and security issues are usually found in the first chakra. Triggers in life that relate to sexual information or empathy are usually found in your second chakra. Triggers that relate to feeling controlled or manipulated are found in your solar plexus, or third chakra. Triggers from the outside world that relate to matters of the heart and compassion are found in your heart or fourth chakra. Outside energies that relate to speaking your truth or lack thereof, are found in your fifth chakra. People, situations or triggers that relate to your ability to see clearly are found in your "third eye", or sixth chakra. And triggers that relate to blocking your certainty and ability to "know things off the top of your head" are found in your "crown" or seventh chakra.

When you are aware of what is going on within you while relating to the outside world, you can use visualization techniques to soothe your self from the effects of the trigger and you can stay emotionally centered. For instance, when you have money issues, you can look into the chakra that pertains to "survival," which is the first chakra, and visualize any number of techniques, such as "removing cords," closing down the chakra, or sending color to the chakra, to help you to soothe your anxiety and to keep you centered.

Removing Cords and Daggers

You can use the technique of visualizing "cords" and "daggers" in order to remove offending energy from your space. "Cords" and "daggers" are beams of energy that you can visualize as coming from an outside source (Bostwick, 1989). They penetrate your bubble and affect a chakra or a specific picture in a chakra. If you know the particular category of an issue that was triggered, you can locate the chakra where the issue resides, and you can visualize the offending source sending you a cord or dagger that hits your chakra. This act helps you become proactive. You can take charge over the energy that could ordinarily control you, because you can now remove the cord with your mind's eye and send it back to its owner.

Using the above example, let's say you have money issues. You would then visualize your first chakra, because that is where the pictures reside that pertain to survival issues. If your coworker causes you to feel insecure about your position in the firm, imagine the cord or dagger that he or she is putting into your first chakra. In your mind's eye, remove the cord and send it back to this individual. When you visualize where the source of your anxiety is coming from and use your imagination to remove the culprit and soothe your self, then you will be able to reach a calmer place emotionally. By doing so, you have healed your anxiety by "performing an operation" on your chakra.

If a coworker is in competition with you and tries to make you feel stupid, consider whether you feel manipulated or controlled (third chakra), or lousy about yourself (fourth chakra and space of affinity for yourself), or whether the coworker is trying to blind you from the truth (sixth chakra and place of clarity). Visualize the "daggers" this person has hurled at you and see which chakras they were sent to. They may have been sent to one or all of them. Decide where you feel vulnerable. This is where the daggers are embedded. Now you can remove them and return them to their owner.

Knowing where the daggers came from and where in your body they were sent gives you the upper hand in the situation. This is so because you become aware of your specific feelings. You are able to "see" the energy that causes you to feel a certain way and can do something about it. You can remove the daggers and soothe yourself, and you can decide whether to confront the source or to observe it with clarity.

Modulating the Chakras

As you may recall, chakras can be seen as vegetable steamers that open and close depending upon a particular situation, or upon your will. Ideally, your chakras will be in balance, which is to say they will be neither too open nor too closed down and constricted. When your chakras are in balance, they allow energy to flow freely through your system and your energy field.

Sometimes a particular situation will trigger your body to open its chakra because it needs more energy from the "universe" in a particular situation. If your body is in immediate danger or in survival mode, such as almost being hit by a car, adrenaline will pump through your body, and you will go into "fight or flight" response. In this case, your first chakra opens wide. If you are in love, your fourth chakra will open wide. If you are being raped, your second chakra will close down. If someone is attempting to brainwash you, your sixth chakra will become blocked and/or closed down.

To soothe your self, you may visualize closing down or opening up your chakras. If you feel anxious, closing down a revved up chakra can soothe anxiety. If your anxiety is related to first chakra issues, visualize closing the first chakra down a bit. If someone is trying to control you, remove the cord they have put in your third chakra and shut it down to a comfortable level.

If a chakra has been shut down due to a bad experience, the goal would be to open it up. For instance, if you have had a painful sexual experience but are now with a "yes" category partner, then visualize opening the second chakra to let in positive energy and to remove the old dagger. If you have had a broken heart from a past relationship, the goal would be to open the heart in order to extricate the daggers.

A more advanced and technical way of opening and closing your chakras is to spin the chakras counter-clockwise to close them down and clockwise to open them up. For more information on the chakra system, I recommend Barbara Ann Brennnan's book, *Hands of Light: A Guide to Healing Through the Human Energy Field,* (1987).

By focusing your awareness on your chakras, you can help heal your self. You can sense which chakras you have shut down or opened up, and you can begin to heal them through visualization.

Sending Color to Your Chakras

Another way to soothe your self when you have been triggered is to visualize sending color to your chakras. If a chakra is depleted of a certain vibration, charging it with a specific color can balance and heal your energy field. If a chakra is too revved up, then bringing in a cooler color can soothe the emotion. If a foreign energy penetrates your space and triggers you, then removing the foreign color and replacing it with another color vibration can soothe your emotions.

As you recall, the color red is associated with the first chakra. Orange is associated with the second chakra, yellow is associated with the third chakra, green is associated with the fourth chakra, blue is associated with the fifth chakra, and indigo is associated with the sixth chakra (Brennan, 1987; Cohen, 1988). The seventh chakra is associated with violet, white (Brennan, 1987; Cohen, 1988) and gold (Bostwick, 1989).

If you are feeling depressed and tired due to issues surrounding survival, such as money concerns, you may want to charge your first chakra with more red. When you visualize bringing in red, you activate your self. This may help pull you out of a listless state. If, on the other hand, you are feeling anxious and overwhelmed about money, then bringing in a cooler color, such as blue, can tone down and soothe your anxiety, because your first chakra may be too revved up.

If someone is invalidating you, look to see what color vibration they have put into your fourth chakra if your affinity for your self is affected, or your sixth chakra if they are warping your reality. Visualize what color this foreign energy feels like to you. For instance, you may feel the color is black or brown or red, etc. You may then remove the color by putting it in a bubble and "blowing it up" and then replacing the space with the color that is in affinity

191

with you and your particular chakra. For instance, you may want to bring in green to your fourth chakra or indigo into your sixth.

Use your intuition to guide you as to what colors you need to soothe and heal your self. There are no "rights" or "wrongs" when it comes to healing your chakras. The important thing is that you are proactively healing your self by visualizing how energy affects you, and you are doing something for your self to soothe your emotions.

"Balancing your chakras with colors" is a wonderful meditation to keep yourself healthy. Visualize bringing into your space the colors that are associated with each chakra. Bring the colors into the respective chakra starting with the first chakra and ending with the crown chakra. Then bring in a golden sun of energy and have the energy permeate every cell of your body and every space in your bubble.

ENERGY AND FAIRY TALE IMAGERY

In the therapy groups and weekend metaphysical retreats that I conduct, I use the imagery of energy and the chakra system to breath life into the emotional and spiritual journeys my clients embark on. I wrote the following fairy tale to help a particular population of women learn to trust their intuition and to "see" with clarity. The story that follows illustrates how you can use your imagination to sense and "see" the energy that surrounds you.

The Blinded Clairvoyant

Far away, in a distant, forested land, there lived a beautiful and fair maiden. One day, as she strolled through the forest, a dashing, strong man, exuding masculine sensuality, caught up to her on his white horse and trotted along beside.

She was immediately attracted to him and his chivalric presence, but he had two strange qualities. As he spoke, clouds came from his breath. And his sensual hands had dexterous daggers for fingers. Nevertheless, she was extremely attracted to him, even though a part of her feared the gentleman's breath and hands. She quieted this cautious voice and followed her heart.

They made passionate love by the moonlight, and his dagger-hands caressed her body as she had never been caressed before. She fell in love. She was swept off her feet and rode with him on his horse.

After a few months, she became increasingly insecure. Twinges and pangs in her heart and stomach increased, and she asked her beau if he had betrayed her with another maiden. "No, no, you insecure woman," he replied, and he threw clouds over her eyes with his words. "You are crazy. Nothing is going on."

She acquiesced, "You are right, my lord." Her gaze looked downward and she became saddened and depressed.

After several days, the twinges and pangs returned. She found a lock of dark hair and a perfumed feather by his bed. She again questioned him. "My lord, have you betrayed me?"

Clouds of smoke blew from his breath and covered her eyes as he again bellowed, "No, no, you crazy, insecure woman! Nothing is going on!" He then threw a dagger into her heart from his dagger-hands -- the very hands that had once caressed her so tenderly.

The dagger felt familiar as it became embedded into her heart. It was the same dagger her father had thrown into her heart when he denied with clouds of breath that he was having a tryst with her mother's closest confidante. It was strange now that she noticed it. Her father had the same breath and hands as her beau.

That night, she had a lucid vision in a dream. She saw herself being burned at the stake. Flames engulfed her as voices shouted, "Witch! Witch!" The pious males from this land were very threatened by the fair maiden. They were threatened by her ability to see the truth and to separate the truth from the lie. They could not blind or control her and were threatened by her ability to teach others how to see clearly. They needed to destroy her.

As she awoke, she opened her eyes and saw the clouds of smoke receding from her view. Once more, she could see clearly. The daggers had been extricated from her heart and she loved herself again.

No longer did she need vindication or validation for her

perceptions or her truth. Her certainty in the truth was all that mattered.

With this epiphany, the clouds in the sky parted and from the heavens, her true love descended to her. She had found her self, and as a result, her earth partner and soul mate had found her.

***

This story is for women (and men) in abusive, controlling or heart-breaking relationships. They have lost their selves and their ability to see a situation clearly (e.g., riding away on *his* horse; being swept off her feet and losing her grounding). They override their intuition and are blinded either by love or dependency.

The story emphasizes the power of unresolved past childhood experiences and their influence upon present day choices in partners. The story goes on to emphasize that knowledge and truth is within an individual, and by listening to feelings (i.e., the twinges and pangs) and by heeding dreams from the unconscious, the person is able to find herself again. Then all is in accord.

Part IV
EXERCISE SERIES

Chapter 20
EXERCISES

The following exercises have been developed to help my clients find their core in various situations. The exercises are designed for you to do in your private time. They assist you in staying solid within your self, and they enable you to become even more familiar with your feelings and with your core essence.

The first exercise, "Handling Projections," assists you in how not to lose your self when people project negative energy into your space. The "Validation Journal" serves as your mirror of positive attributes, and enables you to strengthen your core. The "Character Sketch/Analysis of Previous Relationships" helps you to analyze patterns of relationship energy that you are attracting into your space and gives you the opportunity to see what patterns you are repeating and what lessons you are learning. Finally, "Your Ideal" and "A Collage of 20 Goals and Wishes" exercises help you to discover and create what you want to manifest in your life. This workbook of exercises will assist you in keeping an internal connection with your core so that you will know your self well.

Handling Projections

The single most important factor in feeling solid within your self is to be in "affinity" with your self and with your feelings. When you know your self well, you are able to validate your feelings, and you are able to trust your self and your truth. You become impervious to energy that attempts to make you feel badly about your self or that tends to make you question your self.

Often times, "no" category people will try to throw you off your center and make you feel badly about your self by finding a vulnerability or "Achilles heel" that makes you doubt your self. They will project their own negative feeling or warped reality about you into your space. If you do not know your self well, you will be susceptible to absorbing their "picture" of you into your space. You will then lose your own reality and truth about your self and end up questioning your feelings.

The following exercise helps you to stay on your center and helps you to validate your own feelings when "no" category energy invalidates you. You will be impervious to the negative energies when you can validate your feelings and see the negative energy clearly.

For the following exercise, you will need a piece of paper or a page in your journal divided into three columns. Label the first column, "Projection," label the second column, "Dispute/Validation," and label the third column, "My 6th Chakra Reality," which is your space of clarity about the situation.

Let's say that someone is in competition with you and is threatened by your ability to accomplish your goals. She may project her own feeling of competitiveness towards you into your space by saying that *you* are in competition with *her*. If you know your self well, then you will be able to validate your self and see her projection of you clearly.

First, you would record her projection of you in the first column of your journal. In this case, you would write the projection, "I am competitive with her" under the first column heading. Next, you would record your truth about your self in the second column under the heading, "Dispute/Validation." In this case, you would validate your self by writing, "I am not competitive with her. I am merely accomplishing my goals and focusing on my own path." Finally, you would record your perception of her feelings/behavior in the third column, labeled, "My 6th Chakra Reality," and see her energy clearly. In this case, you might write, "She is in competition with me and is triggered by me, perhaps because achieving my goals makes her feel insecure about herself."

When you process your feelings using this method, you will successfully keep an individual's negative projection about you out of your space. You will stay in affinity with your self by validating your self and by seeing the situation clearly.

The following example illustrates a situation where this exercise was applied. My patient came from a dysfunctional home. One stepbrother was a hard-core drug addict. He tried to hide his addiction from the parents by lying and spreading rumors about my patient to the parents in an attempt to deflect suspicion onto someone else. Meanwhile, my patient's sister was in competition with my patient. This sister was also addicted to alcohol and prescription drugs but tried to deflect the suspicion off herself and on to my patient by lying to the parents about my patient. The parents were blinded by these two siblings. They believed the lies about my patient, and they shunned her.

During the time the lies were spread, my patient was a beautiful and accomplished person who was an undergraduate in pre-med. While she may have had some alcohol at sorority/fraternity parties and smoked cigarettes while she was studying, she had never been addicted to drugs and maintained a 4.0 grade-point average. She was heart-broken and irate that her parents could abandon her and be so blind as to believe the horrible things that were being said about her.

I began to see this patient while she was putting herself through medical school at a prestigious university. During the course of our work together, the truth came out about her siblings. The stepbrother was arrested for dealing cocaine. The sister's third husband divorced her and took custody of their children. The sister's alcoholism had progressed to the point where she was fired from her job and arrested for drunk and disorderly behavior. In short, the siblings hit bottom. They finally got help and started the process of recovery but never apologized to my patient.

The dilemma for my patient began when the family wanted her to celebrate Passover with them. My patient decided not to go to the family function because she did not want to be around "no" category energy that had destroyed her reputation and her connection to her parents. The parents and family then projected on to my patient that she was "immature and selfish" for not being able to get over her hurt and be part of the family. In order not to let these projections invade her space and throw her off her center, she preformed the "Handling Projections" exercise.

First, she listed the projection under the first column and wrote, "I am immature and selfish." In the "Dispute/Validation" column she wrote, "I am centered and mature, and I am loving towards benevolent, "yes" category people. I chose to surround myself with loving energies who respect and see me clearly." In the third column, under the "6th Chakra Reality" heading, she wrote, "These siblings were threatened by my ability to see through them clearly and were insecure enough to want to destroy my reputation. My parents favored these siblings and chose to abandon me in order to continue to view their favorites in a good light."

After completing the exercise, my patient felt vindicated for setting her boundary and for protecting herself from harmful energy. Rather than allowing the projections to invalidate her and make her lose her boundary, she was able to see the situation clearly. As painful as it was, she was able to tolerate the sadness of not being connected to her family. She had maintained her boundary and had maintained her feeling of solidness. This was a far superior feeling to that of acquiescing, overriding her anger and losing her self in order to hold out for an impossible connection with her family.

Another patient of mine was a chiropractor. She worked hard to establish her practice and enjoyed the finer things in life, such as travel, gourmet dining and wearing designer clothing. One of my patient's colleagues was in competition her and felt disdain towards my patient for being successful and fashionable. This colleague told other colleagues that my patient was superficial, was only interested in making money, and did not care about the disadvantaged and the poor.

In order for my patient not to absorb the projections, she completed the "Handling Projections" exercise. Under the "Projection" column she wrote, "I am superficial, only interested in making money, and don't care about the disadvantaged and the poor." Under the second column, she disputed the projection and validated herself, saying, "I enjoy the fine things that life has to offer. I love travel, good dining and beautiful clothing and surroundings. I have worked hard to be able to enjoy these things. I do care about the disadvantaged and poor community or else I would not have become a healer. Five percent of my practice is "pro bono" and I accept much lower fees for a large percentage of my clients who would otherwise be burdened because of their insurance plans." In the third column, she saw her colleague with her centered perception and wrote, "My colleague has different tastes than I have. Neither of us is right or wrong. She is misinformed about my practice and is not familiar with my heart and my integrity." Using this exercise, my client was able to validate herself and like her self. She was able to "agree to disagree" with her colleague's tastes, instead of feeling badly about having tastes for the finer things in life.

Use this exercise to maintain affinity with your self. If a projection really triggers you, then be able to see whether the comment or the jab has some truth or merit to it. But be cautious about losing your self to someone else's perceptions/distortions of you. As long as you can validate your self and see the other person clearly, you will be at peace with your self and will feel solid and centered.

The Validation Journal

The validation journal serves as your mirror to reflect back to you all of your positive qualities, contributions and accomplishments. It produces "yes" category energy that validates who you are when you need to be reminded of your positive characteristics and loving heart.

The validation journal affirms who you are. The journal is a collection of tangible things you have done or achieved in your life. It also records positive reflections of you that have been made about you by others. You are able to "let in" the positive reflections easier than if you were to merely recite affirmations to yourself because the journal is comprised of real things you have done in your life and real things people have said about you.

To compile your journal, you will need a blank, three-ringed binder. For part of the binder, you will need plastic sheets so that you can insert documents and letters into the pages. For other entrances, you will need access to a copy machine, a glue stick, and scissors so that you can paste things into your journal. And for another part of the journal, you will need pages of paper so that you can write entrances into your journal.

Every one of your achievements will be entered somewhere in your journal. Photocopies and pictures of awards you have won from childhood through adulthood will be placed in your journal. Acceptance letters for schools, organizations, and jobs will go in your journal. Pictures of diplomas and projects you have completed, such as a chair you have made or your undergraduate thesis, will be photographed and placed in your journal.

In another section of your journal, you will want to record the positive things that people have said and felt about you. For instance, letters of recommendation, positive work reviews, Thank You notes, love letters, birthday cards, and letters of appreciation all will go in your journal. You will also want to write an ongoing list of compliments people have made to you and enter them regularly in the pages of your journal. For instance, if your boss says how "brilliant" your presentation was, or if a student says that you're the "best," then write an ongoing list of these comments in your journal.

In yet another section of your journal, you will keep an ongoing list of things you do for others that comes purely from your heart. For instance, under the ongoing section that lists "random deeds of kindness," if you give a friend flowers to cheer her up, record that heartfelt deed in your journal. If you give money to your favorite charity, record that deed in your journal. As long as the deed is purely motivated by your heart and *not* because you want to feel good about yourself so that you can have something to record, then you should record the deed in this journal.

Finally, you can paste photographs in your journal of events in your life where you have felt loved and validated. For instance, if someone gave you a surprise party, then put that picture of the party in your journal. If someone gave you a gift of love and it was recorded on photograph or documented with a ticket stub, etc., then you can place the memory of the event in your journal.

As you compile this validation journal, you will be able to surround yourself with a concentrated form of loving, supportive energy, and you will be reminded of your positive and loving self. When you are feeling down, this journal can be your greatest ally.

Analysis of Relationship Choices and Patterns

Many years ago, I created this exercise for a women's retreat I conducted on relationships. Over the years, I have found this exercise to be a useful tool for both my male and female clients to help them see patterns and/or growth from one relationship to the next.

This exercise is usually suggested after one relationship has ended and before another begins. It is used for enabling a person to see patterns in their overall relationship history and to be able to make better choices in partners in the future.

To complete the following exercise, you will need to make one copy of the exercise for each significant relationship in your past that you want to analyze. You can complete the form for each relationship in any order, for instance, starting with your most recent relationship or your earliest relationship. However, after you have completed the forms for all your significant relationships, you will want to spread them out in front of you in chronological order so that you can assess your patterns and growth over time.

CHARACTER SKETCH/ANALYSIS OF PREVIOUS RELATIONSHIPS

Name_____

Dates: From_____to _____

How did the relationship begin? (Who picked whom?)

Physical characteristics (Height, hair color, body-type (for male partners; facial/chest hair, etc.) (For female partners; voluptuous, petite, etc.)

His/her personality (sociable, a loner, sarcastic, no sense of humor, gregarious, warped, strange, etc.)

His/her temperament (explosive, shy, moody, even-keeled, etc.)

His/her core personality make-up (passive-aggressive, narcissistic, depressive, flip-flopper, manic, etc.)

How much of your personality was stifled when you were around him/her?

1 2 3 4 5 6 7 8 9 10

To what extent did you feel controlled? In what way?

1 2 3 4 5 6 7 8 9 10

How much did you feel engulfed versus allowed your freedom?

1 2 3 4 5 6 7 8 9 10

What type of relationships did he/she have with his/her family? (Stable, dysfunctional, close, estranged, etc.)

Alcohol/Drugs/Cigarettes/Eating Disorder/ Gambler/Workaholic, etc.?

Educational level/Aspirations?

Career choice?

Finances and way with money?

How did he/she communicate with you on a sexual level?

How did you feel about yourself sexually when you were with him/her?

Was he/she faithful? Were you the only person on his/her mind sexually?

How free were you to express your true feelings with him/her?
1 2 3 4 5 6 7 8 9 10

How was the communication on an idea/intellectual level?

How was the communication on a spiritual/soul level?

How did the relationship end? Who broke up with whom?

Did you abandon your self in this relationship? How? (E.g., by not setting space boundaries, sexual boundaries, allowing him/her to sway your own truths so that you lost your certainty, acquiescing to drugs/alcohol to "join" him/her, etc.)

Why did the Universe put him/her in your life? What life path lesson(s) did you learn as a result of going through this relationship?

What part of you (if any) is still left in past time in this relationship? (Sometimes it feels like a piece of you has "died," e.g., trust, innocence, enthusiasm . . .)

In what way did this relationship teach you or disclose truths to you about your father/mother? (Sometimes we attract a similar vibration to that of our parents in order to learn more about our parents as people.)

Finding Your Core: Your Deepest Desires

The following exercise on "Ideals" was created by me many years ago for a women's retreat I conducted on "Manifesting your Dreams." I have found this exercise to be useful in helping clients remove any blocks they may have in dreaming and creating for themselves. It also helps them find their core essence and desires.

The only requirement for this exercise is to *not* limit yourself or talk yourself out of your desires. Simply allow your imagination to create with no "holds barred."

YOUR IDEAL RELATIONSHIP, CAREER, DREAM HOUSE, AND TRAVEL DESTINATION

Have fun with this exercise! It is meant to open the channels of communication between you and your innermost Self.

When we become in touch with our likes and our essence, we begin to reclaim our certainty. We begin to trust our perceptions and intuition. And we begin to allow ourselves to have and to receive.

For this exercise:

Take a few minutes of uninterrupted quiet time to be in your thoughts and to create. Run a hot bubble bath and fix yourself a cup of tea or coffee (and put it in a beautiful china cup or your favorite mug). Or, find a beautiful spot outdoors under the moonlight. Or, sit by the ocean, bay or lake, have your favorite soda with you, and pour it in a beautiful glass or goblet. You get the idea!

Now, turn the page and allow your imagination to create. Do not limit yourself or talk yourself out of your desires . . .

YOUR DREAM RELATIONSHIP

What personality characteristics does this person have?

What does he/she look like?

How does this person make you feel when you are with him/her?

How do you feel about life when you are with him/her?

What does the communication feel like on a feeling level?

What does the communication feel like on an idea/intellectual level?

How does he/she communicate with you on a sexual level?

How do you feel with him/her when you are with him/her sexually?

How is the communication on a spiritual/soul level?

YOUR DREAM CAREER/WORK SPACE

What is your dream career?

How do you feel about yourself when you imagine yourself doing this type of work?

What makes this work fulfilling?

How much money are you making in this career?

YOUR DREAM HOUSE

What style architecture is this home?

What materials is it made out of?

Where is it built? (i.e., on the ocean, up on a hill, overlooking a lake, in a canyon, etc.)

Where is the house located?

What does the kitchen look like? (e.g., marble counters and floors, brick, hanging copper pots and plants, contemporary with a gourmet island, etc.)

What does the living room look like? How will you decorate it? (I.e., cathedral ceilings with floor to ceiling windows, hardwood floors and oriental throw carpets, wall-to-wall carpeting, contemporary, antique, stone fireplace, skylights, waterfall, etc.)

What does the master bedroom look like? (I.e., fireplace, Jacuzzi, etc.)

What does the entry hall look like? (I.e., Fourier with sweeping spiral staircase, black and white tile with one large piece of sculpture, waterfall, etc.)

YOUR DREAM TRAVEL DESTINATION

What country have you always wanted to visit?

What is it about this country that intrigues you?

How will you travel to this country? (E.g., by airplane, cruise ship, car, etc.)

How will you travel when you are in this country? (E.g., by airplane, barge, train, car, horse, donkey, hiking on foot, etc.)

How long will you stay in this country?

A Collage of Twenty Goals and Wishes

This exercise enables you to get in touch with your core desires and essence. It is fun to create and get to know what you truly like when no limitations are placed upon you. Have fun creating and getting to know your self!

The following exercise invites you to make a list of twenty goals you would like to accomplish and/or wishes you would like to have. Do not stop until you complete all twenty goals and/or wishes, even if it takes you a couple of days to complete. Do not limit yourself, no matter how ridiculous or far-fetched a wish is. For instance, if you want to fly to Jupiter, then put it down on your list. If you want to travel to the bottom of the ocean, then list the wish. You may also find yourself repeating and listing a wish twice or more times. This usually happens when a desire to accomplish or have something is particularly strong.

After your list is finished, cut out pictures of images from magazines that represent your goals and wishes. You can also draw a series of images that represent your goals and wishes.

Now superimpose the pictures and paste them on paper to make a collage. You can then place this collage in your journal. The collage helps to keep the wishes alive, and enables the creative energies to work towards manifesting your dreams.

Chapter 21

EPILOGUE:

A SPIRITUAL PHILOSOPHY ON FORGIVENESS

The supreme destination and ultimate achievement is to have your heart opened to all. If you are present in your body and if you situate your self behind your semi-permeable bubble-shield, you will be impervious to the negative energies that surround you. Your heart chakra will be open, enabling energy to flow through your system.

From this space, you can observe the world with acceptance and grace as you allow every soul to be just where they are on their path towards wholeness and enlightenment. This is the space that the Masters, such as Christ and Buddah, reached. This is the stance that enables one to achieve inner peace.

Let's suppose, however, that you are in a situation where you are not centered behind your semi-permeable bubble and that you are not able to deflect a negative energy from hurting you. If someone violates your boundaries and causes you pain, you may feel hurt, angry or resentful.

The Oxford American Dictionary defines the verb, "forgive," to mean "to cease to feel angry or bitter towards (a person) or about (an offense)," (Erlich et.al., 1980). When you feel angry or bitter, your heart chakra closes down, causing your energy to become blocked. You are not in a state of peace when your heart is shut down.

If someone violates your boundaries and causes you pain, and if they have an awareness of their offensive behavior and are truly remorseful, then it becomes easier to open your heart to them. If someone apologizes to you from their heart, then they are on their way to becoming a "yes" category person.

When you forgive a "yes" category person who hurts you, the stance of forgiveness would be conceptualized as having your heart chakra return to an open position towards that person. It will feel safe to you to forgive this person and to open your heart to them again because they are now aware of your boundaries. It will feel to you as though they will not consciously or unconsciously try to hurt you again.

It becomes increasingly difficult, however, to forgive someone who is unaware of his/her ill-intended or mean-spirited behavior, or who sadistically tries to hurt you. These people are likely to continue to cause you pain in the future because they are unaware of themselves and/or they have strayed from their path and are lost.

Having built your bubble-shield, if you find yourself *not* feeling safe enough to open your heart chakra wide and to forgive someone for his/her infraction on your boundary, it is probably for a reason. This person may be in the "no" category, and may still feel unsafe to you. If you forgive him/her and open your heart wide, then you may feel like you are abandoning your self or overriding your feelings and intuition about this person. You may sense that he or she could consciously or unconsciously cause pain to you in the future. You could also feel as though you are letting them "off the hook" if you forgive them, in which case you would still feel resentment or anger towards them anyway. If your heart is closed to the offender, however, then *you* are the one who is suffering, because your heart will be blocked, inhibiting energy from flowing freely through your system. You cannot be fully at peace if your heart is closed.

If a "no" category person violates your boundaries and causes you pain, the alternative stance of forgiveness would be to conceptualize your heart chakra as open half way into what can be considered a neutral stance towards that person. Your heart is neither closed down and angry/bitter, nor is it opened wide and in a state of vulnerability. Energy still flows through the chakra when your heart is in a neutral, half opened position, and you can still be at peace internally.

Sometimes it is difficult, if not impossible to heal from the wounds others have inflicted until, or unless, the offenders recognize their behavior and give you their heartfelt apology. But if they never arrive at this space of awareness, how can you heal your pain? How can you find inner peace and reach a space of forgiveness and acceptance?

I have come to adopt a spiritual philosophy that helps with the healing process in this case. While the following philosophy has been held by spiritualists for more than two thousand years, several beautifully written and well researched texts have been published recently to explain what happens to our souls after we leave the physical plane. One of my favorite works on this subject is Michael Newton, Ph.D.'s book, *Journey of Souls – Case Studies of Life Between Lives*, (1994). Dr. Newton uses hypnotherapy to regress his clients. He presents twenty-nine cases to illustrate the ongoing existence of our souls between incarnations and to expound upon the lessons and purposes of our souls' journey. Another wonderful book researching past life existence is Yale medical school graduate, Brian L. Weiss, M.D.'s, *Many Lives, Many Masters*, (1988).

I believe that we are eternal souls, and that we incarnate on earth to learn lessons about love and life. Each lifetime presents a series of lessons for us to learn, and these foster our soul's growth and evolution towards "the Light" and towards love.

After we leave our physical bodies and move into the Hereafter, we drop our veil of ignorance and are able to review the lessons we were to learn and gauge our progress in that lifetime (Newton, 1994). If a soul has not learned a lesson about love and life in the physical body, and if a soul causes pain towards another, the soul will have awareness about this misguided behavior in the Hereafter. The soul will then have to repeat the lesson in another reincarnation in order to grow and advance along the path (Newton, 1994).

To ease the pain from a lost soul's misguided behavior, I offer the following process. In a space of meditation, imagine the eternal, Higher Self of the person who has violated you. Visualize their Higher Self apologizing to you from their heart. Imagine them being fully aware of the pain they have caused you and see their love for you in their eyes. Allow your self to feel this apology. Allow your self to feel their compassion for your pain.

If you can shield your self from their negative energy on the physical plane and if you can recognize that they are not very far along the path towards perfection, then you can accept these souls for where they are, spiritually. You do not have to like them or agree with their behavior. Yet from this space, you can open your heart to them from behind your protective shield and have compassion for a fellow soul who is spiritually young and not very far along on the way.

If you do not subscribe to this spiritual philosophy about transcendence and awareness in the Hereafter, then I offer an alternative perspective on healing . . .

We are all here on this planet for soul growth and evolution. Some are not as far along on the path as others. These people commit major violations against other people's boundaries, such as rape, incest and homicide. Their souls are lost, and the Karma they incur is enormous.

If you can do your best to shield your self from their energies, then that is all you can do. Sometimes, you may actually be the recipient of this horrific energy. If there is a life beyond this physical plane, then the Karma that is incurred on the planet will still be in place in the Hereafter, and the offender will have to face the inevitable backlash that must result from what he or she has done. "What goes around comes around." "A man reaps what he sows." These are universal truths.

The ill-conceived actions will undoubtedly cause the victims or their survivors immense pain. If we can adopt a philosophy that some of life's greatest lessons are learned through pain, then the pain that atrocities have caused may actually further the soul growth of the victims. The victims will grow through feeling, mourning and grieving their pain. They will develop profound compassion for their pain, and hence open their hearts to themselves. And it is through the love of one's self that one is able to develop compassion for others and a greater love for humanity.

BIBLIOGRAPHY

Baker, Howard S., & Baker, Margaret. "Heinz Kohut's self psychology: An overview." *American Journal of Psychiatry,* 1987; 144 (1): 1-9.

Berne, Eric. "Transactional analysis: A new and effective method of group therapy." *American Journal of Psychotherapy,* 1958; 12: 735-743.

Bostwick, Lewis. Founder: The Berkeley Psychic Institute. Classes attended at the Berkeley Psychic Institute, Berkeley, CA, 1989.

Bradshaw, John. *Bradshaw On: The Family – A New Way of Creating Solid Self-Esteem* (2nd edition). Deerfield Beach, Fla.: Health Communications, Inc., 1996.

Brennan, Barbara Ann. *Hands of Light – A Guide to Healing Through the Human Energy Field.* New York: Bantam Books, 1988.

Cohen, Neil S. *Chakra Awareness Guide – Understanding and Activating the Body's Seven Main Energy Centers.* Mount Shasta, CA: Legion of Light Products, 1988.

Ehrlich, Eugene; Flexner, Stuart Berg; Carruth, Gordon; & Hawkins, Joyce M. *Oxford American Dictionary.* New York: Oxford University Press, Inc., 1980.

Gay, Peter. *The Freud Reader*. New York: W.W. Norton & Company, Inc., 1989.

Hay, Louise L. *You Can Heal Your Life*. Carlsbad, CA: Hay House, Inc., 1984.

Hewitt, William W. *Beyond Hypnosis – A Program for Developing your Psychic and Healing Powers*. St. Paul, MN: Llewellyn Publications, 1991.

Hunt, Dr. Valorie, Massey, W., Weinberg, R., Bruyere, R., and Hahn, P. "Project Report: A Study of Structural Integration from Neuromuscular, Energy Field, and Emotional Approaches." U.C.L.A., 1977.

Mahler, Margaret S. "On the first three subphases of the separation-individuation process." *International Journal of Psychoanalysis*, 1972; 53(3): 333-338.

Masterson, James F. & Rinsley, Donald B. "The borderline syndrome: The role of the mother in the genesis and psychic structure of the borderline personality." *International Journal of Psychoanalysis*, 1975; 56: 163-177.

Miller, Alice. *The Drama of the Gifted Child: The Search for the True Self*. New York: Basic Books, 1981.

Miller, Michael L. "Validation, interpretation, and corrective emotional experience in psychoanalytic treatment." *Contemporary Psychoanalysis*, 1996; 32(3): 385-410.

Bibliography

Newton, Michael. *Journey of Souls: Case Studies of Life Between Lives.* St. Paul, MN: Llewellyn Publications, 1994.

Pinneau, Samueal R. The infantile disorders of hospitalism and anaclitic depression. *Psychological Bulletin,* 1955, 5; 429-452.

Seligman, Martin E.P., and Maier, Steven F. "Failure to Escape Traumatic Shock." *Journal of Experimental Psychology,* 1967; 74: 1-9.

Wiess, Brian L. *Many Lives, Many Masters.* New York: Simon and Schuster, 1988.

Wu, Jenai. "Beauty and the beast: A myth of sadness, madness, and hope in anaclitic depression." *Psychoanalytic Review,* 1997; 84(3): 365-380.

INDEX

ABOUT THE AUTHOR

Alisa S. Burgess, Ph.D. is a licensed clinical psychologist in private practice in San Francisco, California. She works extensively with adults and couples, specializing in individuation and relationship issues.

In addition, Dr. Burgess is the Group Therapy Program Director in the Student Health Center at San Francisco City College. She is a primary clinical supervisor for post-doctoral candidates serving internships at the college. She is also a guest lecturer on the college campus.

Dr. Burgess graduated with Honors and Distinction from The University of California at Berkeley. She received her doctorate degree in clinical psychology from The California School of Professional Psychology in Berkeley/Alameda. She is a member of the Northern California Society for Psychoanalytic Psychologists.

Dr. Burgess is also a graduate from the Berkeley Psychic Institute in Berkeley, California, where she received extensive clairvoyant training in metaphysics and the healing arts. She has conducted numerous workshops and weekend retreats, bridging metaphysical, spiritual and psychological topics. Dr. Burgess brings fifteen years of clinical experience and spiritual training to her work.

Alisa S. Burgess, Ph.D. resides in Tiburon, California.

For more information about Dr. Burgess's private practice, appearances and workshops, please visit her Web site, www.AlisaSBurgessPhD.com

m8042-C
42 TD